MT EVEREST: CONFESSIONS OF AN AMATEUR PEAK BAGGER

BY KEVIN FLYNN

WITH GARY FALLESEN

HAYSTACK PRESS

PITTSFORD, NEW YORK

Mount Everest: Confessions of an Amateur Peak Bagger
By Kevin Flynn with Gary Fallesen

Published by:
Haystack Press
175 Sully's Trail, Suite 100
Pittsford, NY 14534, U.S.A.

orders@haystack-press.com
www.haystack-press.com
www.everestconfessions.com

All photos by the author unless otherwise credited.
Cover photo: Taken on May 15, 2005. Shows several climbers taking a break on Everest's South-East Ridge at about 27,800 feet.
Back cover photo: Kevin Flynn at Camp 1. Photo courtesy of Brien Sheedy.
Cover Design by Martino Flynn, LLC
Edited by RK Edit

ISBN print ed.   0-9767431-3-2
Library of Congress Control Number: 2005930199

Publisher's Cataloging-In-Publication Data
(Prepared by The Donohue Group, Inc.)

Flynn, Kevin, 1957-
   Mt. Everest : confessions of an amateur peak bagger / by Kevin Flynn ; with Gary Fallesen.

   p. : ill. ; cm.
   ISBN: 0-9767431-3-2
1. Mountaineering expeditions--Everest, Mount (China and Nepal)
2. Everest, Mount (China and Nepal)--Description and travel. I. Fallesen, Gary. II. Title. III. Title: Mount Everest.

GV199.44.E85 F59 2006
796.5/22/092   2005930199

CAUTION: High altitude mountaineering is extremely dangerous. Severe injury and death are both possible. This book is in no way intended as instructional. The author and publisher assume no responsibility or liability for any injuries or accidents incurred from using this book.

While the author has made considerable attempts to make this book as accurate as possible, errors may exist.

*To my wife Maggie
who made coming home
the best part of climbing
Mount Everest.*

ABOUT THE AUTHORS

Gary Fallesen and Kevin Flynn on the summit of Mt. Kilimanjaro

Kevin Flynn is one-third owner and partner in the marketing communications firm Martino Flynn, LLC, one of the fastest-growing firms in Western, NY. Aside from Kevin's duties as partner, he also develops creative strategy, services accounts, and supervises the media, account services and new business functions of the agency.

Kevin has great passion for hiking and mountaineering. He is a two-time Adirondack 46er (someone who has climbed the 46 peaks that are 4,000 feet or higher) and has climbed and hiked throughout the Northeast.

Kevin expects to climb the "Seven Summits"—the highest peak on each continent. To date, he has climbed Mt. Everest (Asia), Mt. McKinley (North America), Mt. Kilimanjaro (Africa), Aconcagua (South America) and Elbrus (Europe). He has Antarctica and Australia left and expects to complete them by 2006.

He has produced two videos on McKinley and Kilimanjaro that have been sold throughout the world. He has also shot video footage on Aconcagua, Elbrus, and Everest and expects to complete more videos in the near future. Kevin has given presentations to dozens of groups about his mountaineering adventures.

Kevin is an instrument-rated, single-engine private pilot. He flies to meet with clients and prospective clients throughout the Northeast. In addition, Kevin volunteers as an Angel Pilot—someone who flies non-critically ill patients and family members to various destinations for medical treatment or visitation.

He also enjoys golf and skiing.

Kevin is on the Board of Directors for the Center for Environmental Information (CEI) and has served in that capacity since 1999.

Married to first wife Maggie since 1990.

◆ ◆ ◆

In 1996, after two decades as an award-winning traditional sportswriter, Gary Fallesen became the outdoor writer at the daily *Democrat and Chronicle* newspaper in his hometown of Rochester, N.Y. One of the first people he contacted was his friend Kevin Flynn, about whom he'd written several stories.

Fallesen had listened to his tales about climbing Denali and Aconcagua and asked him "Why?" He didn't understand why Flynn climbed. Gary wanted to go climbing with Kevin in New York's Adirondack mountains and find out for himself what mountaineering was all about. Kevin agreed, but then his plans changed: he was going to climb Mount Rainier instead.

Gary didn't know any better. He had no idea Rainier was 9,000 feet higher than the highest Adirondack peak. Gary went to Rainier with Kevin, Gary Smith and Garry Haltoff, all experienced climbers. Despite suffering altitude sickness, Fallesen fell in love with climbing. Two years later, Kevin and Gary climbed Kilimanjaro. In 2001, Gary attempted Aconcagua with Kevin in Argentina. Fallesen has since become the founding president of Climbing For Christ, Inc., an international non-profit ministry (www.ClimbingForChrist.org).

Climbing has become an integral part of Gary's life. He counts Kevin as one of his closest climbing partners and has enjoyed the trips together and those journeys that they have shared from afar.

Flynn taught Fallesen about FWA (Full Wife Approval) for which his wife, Elaine, is also grateful. She and their two children, Jesse and Hayley, have been a blessing as Gary's support team. They all enjoy hiking and climbing together. This project with Kevin is Gary's second book. Fallesen was honored that Flynn asked him to contribute to this project.

ACKNOWLEDGEMENTS

So many people have helped me along the way in the mountains as well as in the writing of this book. At the risk of leaving a few of these folks out, I'd like to publicly recognize at least some of them.

My business partners Chris Flynn and Ray Martino who support my mountaineering dreams and endure my occasional long absences from the business. Ray provided valuable insight and editing suggestions throughout the writing process. All my friends at work for their support, but especially: Tim Downs, Paul Hill, Frank Piacitelli, Matt Conn, Scott Wolf, Niki Duncan, Mary Pat Brunson, Anne Trabold, Amy Lancaster, Lisa DeRomanis, Elizabeth McDade and Joe Reganbogen, who helped with cover design, layout, journal transcription and all kinds of other support.

All of my climbing buddies along the way. Thanks to Steve Rohrbach, David Greer, Roy Murdough, Garry Haltof, Doug Taylor, Forest McMullin, Nick Parker, Russ Patrick, Gary Smith, Brian Mark, James Dowling, Mark Holbrook, Gary Fallesen and many others with whom I've shared a rope or trail.

To my friends at International Mountain Guides: Eric Simonson, Phil Ershler, Mark Tucker, Dave Hahn, Jake Norton and Jason Tanguay—simply the best in the business.

To all my Everest teammates from 2002: Phil and Susan Ershler, Ted Wheeler, Stuart Smith and Dr. Lee Meyers. Plus the Ford Women's Expedition Team and their supporting guides and team. To all my Everest teammates from 2004: Brien Sheedy, Dan Barter, Ron Hauglin, Khoo Swee Chiow, Mike Donahoo, Will Cross, Brad Clement, John Matthews and Bruce Bramhill.

A huge thanks to all of the Sherpas who helped us up the mountain. Especially to Ang Passang, our Sirdar for both trips. I truly owe Mingma Tshering Sherpa from Phortse a huge debt of gratitude. He was *the* man on my summit day.

To all of the people of Nepal, I thank you for allowing me to be a guest in your country. I hope peace and prosperity return to the kingdom soon.

Thanks to Luanne Freer and her Everest Base Camp Medical Staff for making me feel better when I needed it most.

Thanks to my climbing and writing companion Gary Fallesen for all of your friendship and writing skills. (If this book is a good read, it's due to Gary. If not, blame me.)

Thanks to my sister Colleen and brothers Kerry and Chris for their support. I dedicate this book to the memory of my parents Jerry and Marie, who were both awesome beyond words.

Finally, I have to thank my best friend and soul mate, my wife Maggie, who supports my dreams.

SUMMER OF '75—
FALLING IN LOVE WITH HIGH PLACES

Unmotivated. Lacking direction. I'd taken the year off after high school to "mature." Translation: party.

When my buddy Steve Rohrbach suggested we go on a backpacking trip to the Adirondack Mountains in the summer of 1975, I was in. Never mind that I didn't know the first thing about backpacking. I had no equipment and no one to help guide me as I bought gear: aluminum external-frame pack without a waist belt, cheesy sleeping bag, and a canvas tent that weighed 50 pounds (or something stupid like that). I met the definition of greenhorn, the product of parents whose idea of roughing it was a night at the Holiday Inn. But I loved the idea of adventure. Always have. I remember being eight-years-old and exploring a small stream behind our house. There were frogs, minnows, crayfish. Wildlife.

I might only wander 300 feet down that creek, but to an eight-year-old boy it was another world.

Those imaginary journeys were about as close as I'd gotten to real travel in the first 18 years of my life. I'd never been west of Cleveland, Ohio. Never flown in an airplane. Mountains were foreign to me. Mount Everest? I knew it was the highest peak on the planet. But it was off my radar. Others have this lifelong dream of climbing Everest. Not me. Everest was in an unreachable, faraway land.

So in August 1975 we loaded up our friend David Greer's red Volkswagen Fastback and the three of us headed for the hills. The High Peaks of the Adirondacks are about a five-hour drive from my hometown of Rochester, N.Y. We set out at night, having barely looked at a map. We had three audiocassettes in the car: two by Steely Dan, *Can't Buy A Thrill* and *Pretzel Logic*, and something by that one-hit wonder Brownsville Station, *Smokin' in the Boys' Room*. We headed out with no particular direction, which wasn't a big deal to me—a guy trying to find himself. Somehow, though, we ended up in the Garden parking lot in Keene Valley, in the middle of a major heat spell. We hiked up to the Johns Brook Lodge, where you could camp in those days. It's only 3½ miles, but to a tenderfoot it felt much farther. We set up camp, and it rained all night. But we made it through that first night, even sleeping with our food in our tents. We had no idea bears could be an issue. I probably used the food bag for a pillow.

The next morning we broke camp and headed up Mount Haystack. At 4,960 feet, it's the third-highest mountain in the Adirondacks range. The guidebook tells you the trail is among the most spectacular in all of the Adirondacks.

It also notes that it's an extremely rugged trail: "a serious undertaking, especially with backpacks."

We climbed with full packs, probably weighing 40 or 45 pounds. David was out of shape at the time (he really slimmed down when he went to college), although none of us was in particularly good shape. "I can't believe this is a vacation," David kept saying. "What are we doing here?" We weren't used to this type of challenge. We had no idea what we were doing. We got to the top of Little Haystack, which isn't even a mountain, and thought we were on the summit of Haystack. We thought that the big mountain next to it was Marcy, the highest peak in the state. Not even close. Someone came along and told us where we were and that the big mountain we were looking at was Haystack. We had to keep going. We were amazed at the slow progress we were making. It's only five miles from the Johns Brook Lodge to the summit of Haystack, but it seemed like forever. This climbing thing was harder than we thought it was going to be.

At about two o'clock in the afternoon we finally made it to the top. It was extremely hot in the trees, probably in the mid-90s. But the summit of Haystack is bald rock and when we popped out of the trees there was a nice breeze and it was probably fifteen degrees cooler. I'd never been above timberline anywhere. All of a sudden, there I was taking in one of the best views in the Adirondacks—the abyss of Panther Gorge and the cliffs of Marcy right before my eyes. I could not believe we were in New York State. It was an epiphany for me. I stood there, awestruck. It was love at first sight.

One reason the Adirondacks were so appealing was because the range was so big and it was wilderness. I'd never experienced that. In my book, that was exotic travel.

Climbing became a part of me right then and there. I made a dozen trips to the Adirondacks in the next three or four years, usually alone because none of my friends were into it. David died in a car wreck a few years after we did Haystack. It was hard for me to climb without thinking of him. When I became an Adirondack Forty-Sixer in 1987, I dedicated my 46th peak to David. I wrote in the logbook that he was the guy I'd been with on my first mountain—and that his spirit has always been with me in these hills. Every mountain I've ever gone on he's been with me in some way, shape or form.

When I started out I didn't even know what the Forty-Sixers were; that there was a club for people who climbed all 46 of the 4,000-foot peaks in the Adirondacks. When I heard about it, I just figured it was a good excuse to go back. I loved being up there, loved getting above timberline. Never in the winter, though. Winter climbing? That was an absolutely stupid idea. Summer climbing was nice. Why suffer? I never imagined that 27 years later I'd be climbing Everest and that two years after that I would stand—in agony, suffering from pneumonia and pulmonary edema—on the summit of the highest peak on the planet.

WHO I AM... AND WHO I'M NOT

I am not Beck Weathers, a guy who sailed the Seven Seas and then said, "Now that I've done that, I'll do the Seven Summits." He was the guy who in 1996 was left for dead, but survived during that awful *Into Thin Air* year on Mount Everest. I was not even thinking of Everest when that happened. I just loved mountains and kept going to bigger places.

I am not Ed Viesturs, a guy who has climbed all fourteen 8,000-meter peaks without oxygen. I'm not a freak of nature. There's no way I would try to do it without oxygen. I'm also not a guy who's going to put up a new, heinous route on some major mountain.

I am a bit of a lister—I like lists. But I never started out with the intention that I would one day climb Everest.

That was not on any list that I was keeping. I am not one who says, "I just went up 14,494-foot Mount Whitney in California; let's go to the Himalayas and climb Everest." Eric Simonson (Simo) of International Mountain Guides says he gets one call a week from someone like that. By the time I got to Everest in 2002, I at least thought I belonged there and could give it a credible shot. Looking back, I don't think I was ready to climb it and be successful—I wasn't mentally prepared. In fact, Simo told me to climb 26,906-foot Cho Oyu first. But to me, it was about time and money. I couldn't afford the six weeks it would have taken to do Cho Oyu before taking 12 weeks off to climb Everest.

Mountaineering parallels two other things in my life: work and flying. In each one, I started out poorly or as a complete novice and worked my way up. I went from feeling trapped in my family's failing advertising business to having more money than I ever thought I would make. I went from being a white-knuckle flyer to owning my own plane. I went from below timberline in New York State to the top of the world.

In other words, I'm a late bloomer. I graduated in the lower 20 percent of a high school class of 270. I was one of those students whom teachers told, "You're a really smart guy. If you applied yourself you could do really well." But I was pretty rudderless. I got letters of rejection from three New York state colleges—Oswego, Plattsburg and Fredonia. The only college I got into, Elmira, I couldn't afford. I didn't have any money. I worked two jobs—grocery stock-boy during the day and waiter in a restaurant at night—while all my friends were partying and having fun. I took one and one half years off from school, trying to figure out what I was going to do. When I decided to go to the Community College of the Finger Lakes (CCFL) in Canandaigua, N.Y., I asked my parents for the money. They said I'd have to pay for it myself. So I kept working full-time while I was going to college.

That's when something happened—for the first time I got excited about school. I was studying environmental conservation. I loved the outdoors. I was getting As. At some point a couple of my professors, Chris White and Marty Dodge, started talking to me about going to a four-year school. One of the places mentioned was Cornell University. That was like the Holy Grail to me, and when I got accepted there I was scared and nervous. I could still hear, "You'll never amount to anything if you don't apply yourself." I graduated with honors from CCFL and went to Cornell. I remember walking around the campus in Ithaca, N.Y. one night. It was the farthest I'd ever lived away from home, about a one and one half hour drive. I moved into the Magic Theater, this vegetarian co-ed co-op, with 12 other people. I was never a vegetarian; all sorts of people lived there—from me to a guy from Beverly Hills who thought all schools had gym floors that opened to swimming pools underneath. As I was walking around Cornell that night all the buildings were lit up and people were playing Frisbee and soccer. I thought I'd died and gone to heaven. But I wondered if I belonged there.

I managed to get a 3.0 grade-point average the first year and made the Dean's List both semesters the second year. That was a pretty big deal to me. I graduated in the spring of 1981 with a Bachelor of Science degree in environmental education. I wanted to be a forest ranger or a nature interpreter. But I found out those jobs paid next to nothing and there was a long line of people waiting to do them. I had a girlfriend at the time who I was madly in love with and she'd been accepted to the veterinary school at Cornell. I didn't know what I wanted to do, job-wise, but I knew I wanted to be near her. So my plan was to move back to Rochester and intern with my dad and sister at the family's advertising business for one year. I was getting paid $25 a week—gas money—which meant I had to keep waiting tables to pay the bills. I didn't care. I was getting some real world experience that would help me get back to Cornell for a Master's degree in Communications. I'd be back in Ithaca—with my girlfriend—starting in the fall of '82. Then my girlfriend dumped me in November of '81. I was crushed. However, I was still jazzed by education. So I went back to Cornell. Alone.

My father, Jerry, was semi-retired at the time and the family needed me to do more at the agency. So, after three semesters, I left grad school unfinished and joined a struggling agency. I didn't want to be there. Jerry Flynn Associates became The Flynn Agency. We had a few good years. Then, all of a sudden, we were losing $5,000 a month. That went on for three years. We were always optimistic, but we were slow learners. My sister, Colleen, wanted to get on with her life. I couldn't blame her, I'd sent out a few resumes myself. I'd finished my Master's degree in 1985 and married my wife, Maggie, in 1990. But the business was collapsing around us.

We brought golfing icon Jack Nicklaus in for an event in 1987. It blew up in our faces. We had bad weather on the day of the event. We lost $40,000. We struggled for another five years. I was personally in debt $25,000. The business was $200,000 in debt. That's when I went to climb Mount McKinley. It was somewhat irrational but I had to step away from things to get a better perspective. There had been many years when I didn't take a vacation. This time I needed *something* to bring some joy to my life. Climbing did that for me. As the great Ed Viesturs has said, "Climb for the fun of climbing and only do it for yourself."

BABY STEPS

I was asked to lunch by three guys—Doug Taylor, Garry Haltoff and Jim Carroll—who were thinking of doing a winter climb in 1988. They brought me in because I was the big Adirondack expert. I thought their idea was ridiculous. But I went along with it.

The first time out was the coldest, I think, that I've experienced to this day. Our thermometers went to minus -25 F. The mercury never got above that. We figure it might have gotten to 45-below at night. We knew it was going to be really cold, but I wasn't properly equipped. I wore wool surplus pants from the Army-Navy store and used big-tail catgut snowshoes. I didn't have a good sleeping bag—it was duck down, not goose down. It wasn't awful to sleep in if it was 20 or 25 degrees. We stayed in an open lean-to. I got up to pee in the middle of the night and I was shivering uncontrollably when I got back in my bag. It took 15 or 20 minutes to warm up. But I can sleep in pretty much anything, so I got some rest. Apparently, my companions didn't. At about three in the morning, Haltoff announced, "There's a movement afoot to get up and go." I think he was irritated that I was able to sleep in the bitter cold. I looked around. I didn't see anyone budging. I said, "There's no movement. It's freezing." The movement was quashed. That was our introduction to winter climbing. We didn't even get up the mountain we'd set out to climb—Colden. But we had a nice hike out and I ended up having a pretty good time. That's when we started thinking about doing Mount Washington in winter. That's a big deal. Mount Washington is notorious for having the worst weather in the world. The warnings there are harsh and appropriate—and most people ignore them. In fact, more people have died on and around Mount Washington than on Everest.

By the time we went to climb there in February 1990 we were getting better. I was a 46er by then; I'd finished in 1987. I'd learned a lot more. To get ready for the winter assault of Mount Washington we went to New Hampshire in October of '89 on a scouting trip. It was fairly nice in the valleys but it was already snowing above timberline. The wind was blowing 55 mph with gusts to about 70. I put my 50-pound pack down at one point and the wind tumbled it end over end. It was really blowing. Cool!

When we went back in February, the weather was questionable. We hiked up from Pinkham Notch to the Hermit Lake Shelters and stayed overnight in a lean-to. There were six to eight inches of snow that night and moderate avalanche danger on the Lion's Head Trail, where we were going. Everyone started waffling. I said, "Wait a minute. It's maybe 10 degrees. It's cold, but not ridiculous." Visibility was about one-eighth of a mile. I suggested that we should at least give it a look. Garry Haltof went along with me. Our other two companions stayed behind. The weather ended up improving throughout the day and that kept us heading up toward the top. It was cold on the summit—maybe 5 degrees with 35-40 mph winds—but for Mount Washington in winter it wasn't horrible. I loved having crampons on my feet; going places easy—a Spider-Man sort of thing. With crampons on my feet and an ice axe in my hands, I felt a sense of power. That's when I thought, "It would be cool to go up Mount McKinley." Then I started getting really jazzed about that. Actually, more than jazzed—you could say I became obsessed.

When I went to McKinley in June of 1992, I thought it was my one shot. I needed something to have success at because I wasn't having success at work. Since I had no big mountain experience, I hooked up with the Anchorage-based guiding service, Mountain Trip. The lead guide was an excellent fellow named Nick Parker. Our team spent 24 days on McKinley. But the weather on the mountain didn't cooperate. We never got above high camp at 17,200 feet. I was absolutely crestfallen. I figured I'd never be able to scrape up the money to go again.

When I came home our business started to turn around. We landed a big account. And although it would take two years to get our business healthy, I knew we were headed in the right direction.

Then in October 1992, some people who were going to McKinley the next year approached me. I joined the team in November and was back on the mountain in May 1993. I never thought I'd be back, but eleven months later I was there.

We were a four-man team—Gary Smith, Brian Marks, Jim Dowling, and me. We paired up, with Gary and I climbing together. When we pulled into high camp the weather sucked. It was *deja vu*. For three or four days it didn't change. I was really peeved. We'd done everything right. Then, finally, we got a perfect day. Fifty yards outside of high camp, I caught a front point on one of my crampons and fell flat on my face—on flat ground. I figured it wasn't a good harbinger. But we made it up to Denali Pass at 18,200 feet, higher than I'd ever gone before. When we got to 18,700 feet, we'd done the hardest part; Gary Smith announced that he needed to go down. Jim looked at me and said, "You take him down." I was a bit of a prick. I slammed my ice axe down. I shouted, "It's not fair. We should go down as a team." I was selfish and considering my own goals. Gary was feeling really bad. I think at this point he started to cry a little and I realized what a dick I was being. I realized how much I liked him. This was the first time we'd climbed together. He was my tent mate. He was my friend. I realized I should take him down. I apologized profusely to him and told him, "Your friendship means more to me than the summit."

Those guys, Brian and Jim, went on and summitted. We went back to the tent at high camp. I was looking for someone else to go with and thinking I might try it solo the next day. Who should pull into high camp at that moment, but Nick Parker—the guide I'd climbed with in 1992.

I asked him sheepishly if he had a little piece of rope for me. "Absolutely," Nick said, "We would love to have you." That night I slept poorly. My breathing was really messed up. But the next day I was feeling great as we climbed up through Denali Pass. I had no ill effects from the day before. I was happy and warm and confident—all good things. Then Nick Parker announced that he was feeling shitty and told us to carry on without him. Nick put me in the lead of one of the two four-man rope teams. All of a sudden I was elevated. When we made it to the top, the joy I felt made my heart burst.

It's difficult to explain why I climb. You know what they say; if you have to explain it to someone they won't get it. All I know is that same joy I experienced when I first climbed Haystack I have felt, to some extent, on every mountain I've climbed. It's cool to be on top. But there's more to it than just reaching the summit.

I have three goals when I climb. First and foremost is safety. Some climbing buddies and I formed the Live-To-Tell-The-Tale-Club. That's a good starting point. You don't want to climb with blind ambition. The "summit-or-plummet" or "summit-or-die" mentality only gets you into trouble. The second goal we set is to laugh a lot. Be a good teammate. We want to have great camaraderie on our climbs. The third goal is to tag the summit. You need the first two to make the third successful, especially the first. But you can't be a cheesedick.

I feel I earned my way up as an amateur peak bagger. I really love the mountains. I love climbing, not because I'll take the hardest routes up stuff, but because of the humor, the people, the places you get to go. I remember flying kites in Pangboche on our way to Everest Base Camp in 2004. Watching the kids play and laugh. That's a big part of it.

I never intended for any of it to get this far. I can still remember sitting in one of Marty Dodge's environmental classes at CCFL. He would take a group of students to Alaska each year. I could never afford to go, but I would look at all of his wonderful photos. He would show these pictures of Mount McKinley and tell of someone he knew who fell to his death. I was thinking, "That kind of climbing is just stupid. Dangling from ropes and climbing on snow and ice—that's nuts." I thought those people were out of their minds. Why would people put themselves in those stupid positions? Just ridiculous.

MAKING THE LIST

Roy Murdough was another waiter at the restaurant where I worked before going to college and during my undergraduate years. We ended up becoming roommates and eventually he saw how much I was enjoying college and he went back to school, too. He also ended up at Cornell. Roy, four or five years older than me, was interested in birds and he invited me to go bird watching with him.

We joined the Canandaigua Alcoholic Birdwatchers Association formed by another friend and waiter, Peter Mulvaney. There were only three of us. We'd wait tables until late at night, stay up drinking and then go out when we heard birds chirping at first light. We would go to swamps and obscure places. It was a good excuse to get outside. I couldn't believe there were that many kinds of birds out there that I hadn't noticed before. Roy taught me that if you looked carefully you could see things that were right there under your nose. Then we got into identifying birds and making a life list.

We went to Point Pelee, Ontario, Canada one May for the spring migration. We wanted to see how many species we could see in one day. We started before sun up and counted until sundown. In one day, we identified 101 species.

As I said, I kind of like making lists. The Adirondack 46ers. The one-day Presidential Traverse, where you go over eleven peaks in the White Mountains of New Hampshire. The Seven Summits. Like many others, I read Dick Bass's 1986 book, *Seven Summits*. I thought that would be really cool to do, but I wouldn't be able to do it. I didn't have the time, money, or ability.

Then, after climbing McKinley in Alaska in 1993 and the 19,340-foot Kilimanjaro in Africa in 1998, some friends and I went to Aconcagua in Argentina. At 22,831 feet, it's the tallest peak in South America. Gary Smith and I had tried it in 1995. I went back in 2001 with Smith and Gary Fallesen. It was a bittersweet climb because the two Garys had health problems and decided to turn back, while I made the summit. Even though they encouraged me to go, I felt guilty being up there without them. When I came down from the summit and made it back to high camp, the first thing I said was, "I'm cured. No more big mountains for me." But the cure didn't take. A few months after Aconcagua, I started thinking, "You did get to almost 23,000 feet. Maybe I could do that next step."

Only after Aconcagua did I really start thinking seriously about the Seven Summits. Everest was the major stumbling block in the way. That next step was going to be a big one.

THE DECISION—
DON'T TELL ANYONE... YET

I was driving to the gym. It had been awhile, probably a couple of months since I'd worked out. It always helped me to have a goal—that motivated me to train. Before I went to Aconcagua in January 2001, I worked out three or four times a week for six months. I took it pretty seriously. But I'd been taking a rest. I was finally on my way back into the gym in March of 2001.

That's when I first, really, thought about going to Everest.

The pain from Aconcagua was far enough away that you forget it. As I was coming down from the summit of Aconcagua, I had a bit of what I would come to know as the Khumbu cough—that high-altitude cough. But you tend to forget the pain and remember the pleasure. If you focused on the pain, you wouldn't go back.

I remember thinking, as I was driving in my car, "It would be awesome to go to Everest."

It is the biggie. The Big E. I decided I wanted to go there for the same reason I'd wanted to go to Cornell University after junior college, for the same reason I wanted to learn to fly in the clouds. It was one of those next-step kind of things.

I'd never been to Asia before. I'd read so much of the literature about Everest—from Hillary's first ascent to *Into Thin Air*. I always liked the idea of being an explorer, even though I knew we weren't exploring. Hillary and Tenzing Norgay walked off the map. But I thought it would be cool to retrace the steps of those who'd gone before me.

It's one thing to have the dream and something else to go after it, to realize it. So I thought about it for a while. I didn't just want to blurt out, "I'm going to go climb Everest." I might as well have said, "I'm going to the moon." I didn't feel qualified. I felt like an amateur. I kept it to myself—just in case I came to my senses because then I'd be embarrassed. I wanted to let it sink in a little bit, let the hook set.

There were obstacles. Time. I'd never been away that long. Money. I didn't know how much it would cost—other than the $65,000 bandied about in *Into Thin Air*, a sum of money that not a lot of people really pay. Then I wondered whom I would go with—or more appropriately, who would go with me?

I let it roll around in my head to see if it would become real. I thought it was pretty audacious. Then I remembered a psychology class I'd taken in college. It was about goals. Some people set goals too low. They don't stretch or push themselves. In some cases, people set unattainable goals just to get approval. But it's something they have no chance of making a reality. I wanted to make sure this was attainable. I tried to project myself on that mountain. I imagined what it would feel like to be in the Khumbu Icefall or on the Hillary Step. What would it feel like to have an oxygen mask on?

I could see myself doing that.

So one day at home, sitting out on our deck, on one of the first nice days of early spring, I floated the idea past my wife. "Gee, honey," I said to Maggie, "you know what? I was thinking about climbing Everest."

She knew it was coming. I guess other people knew I was going before I knew. My brother, Chris, said he knew I was going after I came back from Mount McKinley in 1993. He said it was because I was a lister. Maggie knew because she was on her way to becoming an Adirondack Forty-Sixer and she knew the joy of being in the backcountry and the joy of getting to the summit of a mountain.

But she wanted to know the details. It's one thing to be there and know how you feel and what the conditions are, and another thing to be at home. The people at home don't have that luxury of knowing what's going on. In some ways, it's harder to be left at home than to be there actually climbing the mountain.

We talked about it and she said OK. I had FWA.

FWA

FWA stands for Full Wife Approval. It's pronounced "fwah." No climb begins without it. FWA is reserved for big mountains. It's something we joke about, "Dude, I got FWA! We're going!" It's like the fun pass.

Maggie and I started dating on June 21, 1989. It was a love-at-first-sight sort of thing. She was physically fit, but not an outdoors girl. I told her how much I enjoyed the Adirondacks. I asked her if she wanted to go backpacking and, when she said yes, I took her to do Macomb, South Dix and East Dix—three trail-less peaks. I know, "What was I thinking?" Sometimes I get ahead of myself. I knew it was a beautiful climb up the rockslide, but I didn't think about what it would be like for someone who had never climbed to actually have to do it.

We got up Macomb and someone else was there who asked Maggie if she enjoyed the hike. She said, "Yeah. It's my first mountain." They said, "What?! He's taking you up a trail-less peak for your first climb?!"

But she thought it was great. It was a hard, long day and she enjoyed it. We went up to the Adirondacks a couple times a year and when she'd climbed twenty or so peaks she said she might as well become a 46er. She never intended to be a 46er. She finished on my first mountain—Haystack—on July 5, 2003. I had a jeweler make up a custom gold charm of the Adirondack 46er logo. I gave it to her on the summit that day.

That's why she appreciated my love for the mountains. She loved them too.

When I floated the idea of doing Everest, she had four stipulations: One, I had to tell her everything. Good, bad, indifferent. She told me, "Don't leave anything out. If you're going to be gone 12 weeks, say it's 12 weeks. Don't sugar-coat it."

Two, I needed to train like a man-possessed. I had to be real serious about it. Before I went the first time, I ended up working out 12 months. Three, I had to upgrade my gear. I'd always been the frugal mountaineer. Everyone always mocked my fluorescent green fleece jacket that I'd gotten in a closeout bin. Something no one would ever wear, let alone buy. I remember meeting guide Craig John in New Hampshire to do some ice climbing work about six weeks before I left for Nepal. He said, "You need two of these and two of those." I said, "Two? Why two of everything?" He said, "Because it's Mount Fucking Everest. You don't scrimp on the biggest mountain in the world. What if something breaks or you drop it in the Icefall; what are you going to do then?" Four, I had to come home. That was the deal. I'm a member of the Live-to-Tell-the-Tale-Club.

We don't have kids so that made the decision easier. If we had kids, I don't think I would have gone. I think the responsibilities would shift to more important things. Not that I'm judging those who climb who have kids. It just would be a harder decision for me to make.

I've had people say, "Everest was your big dream—what if Maggie said 'no'?" I tell them, "I wouldn't have gone." It's that simple. I can go fly in the clouds, but I also have a motorcycle license from my days in college. I've asked Maggie about getting a motorcycle and she wasn't wild about the idea. We talked about risk and concluded that it's harder to manage on a motorcycle than when flying an airplane or climbing a mountain. So I don't ride a motorcycle. It's a risk-management issue.

The first test for our deal came when I got the Body Disposal Election Form. You have to decide, "If I die on Mount Everest, I prefer to be left on the mountain, to be cremated, or repatriation." I've thought about the possibility of dying on a big mountain. For instance, when I first went to Mount McKinley in June 1992, 11 people had already died on the mountain that year. It made national news. On my way to Alaska I read an article in *Newsweek* saying it was nastier than Everest. People were dying left and right.

So when you look at the Body Disposal Election Form, there's a bit of, "Holy shit!" to it. You start thinking, "What have I gotten myself into?"

The wording is pretty straightforward: "If you die on the mountain, your body will be put in a crevasse and/or marked with a rock cairn in a respectful manner by your Expedition team members...."

"If you die down low, it might be possible to get your body down where it could be cremated by Buddhist monks from the local monastery. This would cost well in excess of several thousand dollars...."

It's definitely something you have to discuss with your spouse. It shows that this is really serious business and was one of the first things that came up after we'd agreed that I was going to climb Everest. I'd been sharing with her who I was talking to about going there and including her in on my e-mails. When I decided I was going with International Mountain Guides, I brought this to her attention.

"Know how I told you I'd share everything?" I asked.

"Yeah," she said.

"Well, here you go," I said, handing her the form. "This is about as serious as it gets. I'm thinking I want my body left on the mountain if I die. What do you think?"

"OK," she said after a moment, "I guess this is one of the things that goes with the territory. Thanks for sharing."

I checked "left on the mountain."

I'M GOING TO CLIMB EVEREST—
NOW WHAT?

From: Kevin Flynn
To: International Mountain Guides (IMG)/
    Eric Simonson
Cc: Maggie Flynn
Sent: Monday, April 30, 2001 12:11 p.m.
Subject: Everest 2002

"Dear Eric,

I am interested in attempting to climb Everest in 2002. I am 44 and in excellent condition. I have been on two expeditions on Denali. Mountain Trip guided the first trip in 1992, where we reached 17,200 feet and spent a stormy week. The second was 1993, when I went unguided with three other guys and we summitted. (I also produced a fifty-minute video on the West Buttress Route, which included my video interview with Bradford Washburn.) I did two unguided trips on Aconcagua on the False Polish Route. The first was 1995 (high camp) and the second was this past January, when we did summit. I did Kilimanjaro in 1998. Plus, I've done Rainier, the Adirondack 46 and numerous winter climbs in the White Mountains in New Hampshire.

Would you consider me for an Everest attempt with my current experience?"

Once you've got FWA, you've got to figure out how you're going to make the climb. You do some research into the companies that go there and you put together your resume. I surfed the Web, checking out sites and seeing what itineraries looked like and what the cost was for various companies. You learn a little about their approaches this way. International Mountain Guides had been in the press in 2001 because they were looking for the body of George Mallory, the British explorer who some argued had been to the top of Everest before dying on the mountain in 1924. IMG was looking for his body and evidence as to how high Mallory had climbed. He was last seen on June 8 of that year climbing toward the summit with Andrew "Sandy" Irvine.

Eric Simonson of IMG had a reputation for being a great expedition leader, a real no-nonsense guy. But the thing that scared me about them on this particular trip was the aspect that their climbers were non-guided. "Non-guided? On Everest?! I can't do that. That's crazy." But, as Simo told me, "If you really need a guide, you probably shouldn't be there."

When I first e-mailed him, he was on the mountain. We

e-mailed back and forth a few times. He never tried to sell me on climbing Everest with IMG. If anything he was pushing the other way. He wanted me to climb something smaller with IMG just to see how everything would go.

From: IMG/Eric Simonson
Date: Tuesday, May 8, 2001 11:11 p.m.
To: Kevin Flynn
Subject: Re: Everest 2002

"Dear Kevin:

While your experience looks great, and I would consider adding you to the team, frankly I'd also really encourage you to consider a climb on Cho Oyu with us before Everest. There are two main reasons for this. First, Cho Oyu gives you a chance to learn the drill with Himalayan climbing. Your Denali experience is great and extremely relevant, but once you hit the 8,000-meter peaks it really is a new ballgame. I hate for people to burn $$ and energy with their beginning Himalayan course on Everest. It's an expensive way to get some valuable learning under your belt. On Cho Oyu, you'll learn the O_2 systems for one thing, and once you strap that stuff on it's like scuba diving for the first time. You'll also learn how to take care of yourself over the long haul up high, as much a mental exercise as anything. Better to be as familiar with the whole deal as possible before going at the Big E. Another reason I'd encourage you to think about Cho Oyu is that it would be a good way for you to see how we run a program and for us to see how you handle yourself on the team and the hill—all before we each commit to a much bigger exercise together. Kind of like a really long first date."

A lot of people in the guiding business would have said, "You've done Denali? Come on, we'll take you." This wasn't a case of, you've got a pulse, you can fog the mirror and you have a checkbook, let's go. If anything, I had to sell myself. I liked that.

From: Kevin Flynn
To: IMG/Eric Simonson
Cc: Maggie Flynn
Sent: Thursday, May 10, 2001 1:39 p.m.
Subject: Re: Everest 2002

"Hi Eric,

I completely agree with your rationale about Cho Oyu before Everest. But my dilemma is time. There's really no way for me to take off as much time as I need to try both summits. The highest I've been is the summit of Aconcagua, which is a far cry from 8,000 meters. I've never strapped on O_2 during a climb so that's totally foreign (I have gone scuba diving, but I doubt that experience transfers at all). As far as mental toughness up high, I have spent 24 days on Denali in '92, 23 days on Denali in '93, 16 days on Aconcagua in '95 and 18 days on Aconcagua in '01. Obviously not nearly as high or long as the Big E, but I feel confident I can do the mental drill."

The fact that I'd been a member of expeditions without guides—McKinley the second time, Aconcagua, Rainier—made me a little more attractive. I was a little more self-sufficient. "Hey, he can cook for himself!"

From: IMG/Eric Simonson
Date: Mon, 14 May 2001 11:13:49
To: Kevin Flynn
Subject: Re: Everest 2002

"Kevin:

Man, I know what you mean about the time. That is THE biggest dilemma for most people, in addition to cost concerns. Let's face it, time and money are in short supply for most of us, and those with jobs have a hard time getting away long enough to do the work on the mountains that we'd like to do. Same for me, believe it or not.

Any chance that you could swing the eight-day Rainier circumnavigation that I am doing in early July? I realize it isn't the same as Cho Oyu, but what it would do is give us a chance to climb together for a few days. You get to know me and see my style, I get to know you and see yours, we talk about Everest, see if it's a good idea. I tell you this, your Denali experience is very good and will serve you well on Everest. Believe it or not, your scuba experience WILL help you, too (I never advertise that, but it's much the same in terms of keeping your wits about you in a life-or-death situation with a bunch of crap on your face, head and chest. If you panic, boom, bad joo-joo)."

We were speaking the same language, even though Simo and I are very different climbers. I would go for a walk around Rainier with him. I felt like I was going on a try-out for that very long first date.

GUESS WHO'S COMING TO DINNER?

The Rainier circumnavigation fell through. No one else signed on. So Simo called and asked me how interested I really was in climbing Everest. When Simo called I was really nervous; it was almost like being interviewed again for college.

"On a scale of 1 to 10, what are you thinking?" he asked me.

"9.5," I said.

"Really?!" Simo said, sounding surprised by my quick reply and the level of my desire to do this thing. "Well, OK, I guess you're on the team."

I remember being pretty excited when I was accepted on the team. It was June. A couple of months later I had a business meeting in Seattle so I arranged to meet Simo and one of his partners at IMG, Phil Ershler. Ershler was going the following year as a non-guided climber. He was climbing with his wife, Susan. They were trying to become the first husband and wife to complete the Seven Summits. This was his second time around. All they had left was Everest. Even though Ershler was a non-guided climber like me, he's *nothing* like me. I felt like I was taking the next step from where I was in my little mountaineering career.

I flew in the night before my business meeting. I killed some time around Seattle. I went to the Marmot store and bought a pair of Everest OneSport boots. I got a closeout deal—$500. I figured that was a steal. It's only $50 a toe. If you bring all 10 toes back, $500 for a pair of boots is pretty cheap.

After shopping, I met Simo and Ersh. Even though I was pretty much on the team, I think they wanted to see me in person. It's one thing to say all these great things about yourself, but if I show up and I'm 5-foot-9, 300 pounds, then they might have an issue. I was kind of nervous about meeting them. There's a little bit of star quality there. Outside of the mountaineering world they're not really known, but inside mountaineering they're highly respected. Simonson is probably the best coordinator in the world for big Himalayan expeditions. They'd found Mallory's body. Simo co-authored a couple of books, *Ghosts of Everest* and *Detectives on Everest*. Ersh was a Seven Summitter. He was in Bass's *Seven Summits* book. These guys were Rainier mountaineering veterans with Simo having led two-hundred-seventy trips and Ersh nearly four-hundred up Rainier. Simo's got another sixteen climbs up McKinley and Ersh has been to the top of McKinley twenty times. They'd turned their passion for climbing into a vocation as guides.

When you meet them, these guys can't be more different. Simonson is this hulking 6-foot-5 dude. He comes across as laidback—"How you doin', man?" But he does not suffer fools gladly. He'll call people out. Ershler, on the other hand, is maybe 5-foot-7 with his crampons on. He's thin, but muscular. He's got a gravelly voice and a twinkle in his eye. He looks as tough as nails, but has a much different manner when he's around people. I would pick up a lot of Ershler-isms when I climbed with him. Things like, "I need that like a moose needs a hat rack." He called backpacks rucksacks, crampons were spikes, and an ice axe was a pig-sticker. While Simo will call you out when you screw up, Ershler can be more client-friendly.

We got together for appetizers and a couple beers. We were talking through it and I was feeling a teeny bit like a deer in the headlights. I was trying to ask intelligent questions. I did not ask, "Do I need a hat?" That's something we joke about. "Nobody told me it was going to be cold. I guess I should have brought gloves."

So they were talking and I was smiling. This was reality. Listening to their climbing philosophy, I could tell I'd picked the right company. We talked about training and oxygen and the Maoist uprising in Nepal. Simo told me not to worry about the Maoists. "If you can survive the mountain," he said, "the Maoists aren't going to get you."

PLAYING LHOTSE FACE IN
NEW HAMPSHIRE

After dinner in Seattle, I was jazzed. Ershler gave me a word of caution, "There's only five months left. Keep training hard. The next thing you know, you'll be getting on the plane for Kathmandu."

He suggested I go to the Mount Washington Ice Climbing Festival in New Hampshire in February and hook up with Craig John, who worked for IMG and summitted Everest in 1998. Even though I had decent mountaineering experience, Everest is approached from the South side a little differently. Where I was used to traveling in roped teams, this route is mostly along fixed lines. You're not roped up with a partner. It's just you and the fixed lines. I felt like I needed training and I wanted to talk gear. The Mount Washington festival offered a two-day Everest prep course. I took Maggie for a weekend of training by day, alone time by night. Knowing you're going to be gone for 12 weeks, with everything speeding up back at home, it was good to have some quiet, down time together.

When I met Craig John I was thinking to myself, "Am I going to be proven a fraud or an imposter? Am I going to measure up?" Then he told me he was going to put me on some stuff that's a bunch harder than the Hillary Step. He said, "That way, when you get there, you're not going, 'Oh, God, this is intimidating.' It's intimidating enough just being at 29,000 feet." We went through my gear—and he made me buy some extra things that I needed. Then we practiced crampon techniques, climbing ice that was steeper than the Hillary Step. Finally, we went to Willey's Slide.

"We're going to go play Lhotse Face," Craig told me.

Willey's Slide is on Mount Willey, a 4,285-foot peak named after the family that was killed by a landslide that swept down the east face of the mountain in 1826. What climbers in the Northeast like about Willey's is that it is roughly the same angle as the Lhotse Face. The Lhotse is an unrelenting 2,000-foot climb above Camp Two on Everest. Willey's isn't as high; it's five or six pitches of ice climbing. But it's good simulation for what you'll find at 22,000 feet on Everest—minus the thin air, of course.

So I put on my sit harness and clipped into about three hundred feet of line that Craig John had fixed for me. I was going to learn to climb Sherpa style, which means you clip a mechanical ascender onto the fixed line and just in front of that—on a separate 6 mm rope also attached to my sit harness—is a safety carabiner. That way you have two points of contact between you and the fixed line. You slide the ascender up the fixed line and you climb up. When you come to an anchor, you remove the carabiner and place it back on the fixed line above the anchor before unclipping your ascender. That way you are connected to the fixed line at all times in case you slip or the wind blows you over. You don't want to slide down the Lhotse Face. Nor, for that matter, do you you want to ride down Willey's Slide.

I was really happy I went to New Hampshire. I was able to talk to another Everest veteran. We talked about the emotional side of the climb. So many people focus on the physical aspects, which are important, but the route on Everest is not the hardest. You need some good, sound technical skills. What people don't talk about is the need for mental toughness and the loneliness issues. You're on the other side of the planet. Even if you decide to go home, it's going to take a week. You think about those things, "Am I going to get homesick? Is my mental toughness strong enough?" That's the great unknown. There are a lot of unanswered questions and the only way to get the answer is to go there.

Craig John told me my climbing skills were good enough to make it. It was fun climbing with him during the day. I had a blast sharing time with Maggie. She would drop me off at school in the morning and pick me up at the end of the day. We'd go out and have a nice dinner and talk. I knew that when we got back home to Rochester, life was going to speed up even more. The next four or five weeks were going to fly by.

IF I MAKE HIGH CAMP, IT WILL BE
A SUCCESS

I did all my weight training at Fairport Fitness, a cavernous gym that usually had only six or eight muscle heads working out. It was dingy. Full of leaks. It felt like a scene out of *Rocky*. I wondered at times if the building was going to implode. It was a real pit. Definitely not a social gym, but what I wanted— a place where I could go, work out and not be distracted by cute girls in spandex or business people chatting up deals. I'd put on my iPod and do my thing: weight training on the arms, abs and legs, and then one to one and a half hours of cardio (stairs, treadmill). I did this three or four times a week for 12 months. I was also running a couple times a week over a great five-mile route that had seven hills.

I'm not a huge fan of working out. I like how it makes me feel, but I'm not a gym rat. So, during workouts, I'd daydream about Everest. That would help me get through the training. I'd read so much about the route I could visualize it. Of course, in my fantasies I was always super strong. People would be surprised to see me go from High Camp to the summit, then all the way back down to Advanced Base Camp in one day. Only a few studly folks could do that. In my mind, I was one of them. At least I hoped I would be. And this was a good way to get in shape for the climb. I'd let my mind wander. Almost always it would circle back to the question: how am I going to do it? The early explorers literally walked off the map, but now you walk off your own personal map.

At times I could see myself doing well; other times I wondered if I belonged there. That led me to thinking that if I could just get to High Camp, the climb would be a success.

Admittedly, I was emotionally and mentally unprepared to get to the top. Simo's comments were in the back of my mind, "You should go to Cho Oyu first. It's a different ballgame up there." Self-doubt started to creep in. It saps a lot of your energy. Yet I knew that climbers far stronger than me had failed to reach the summit, and it made me wonder, "What right or chance did an amateur peak bagger like me have at making the top?"

I don't think I was ready to succeed on Everest. Goal setting sometimes limits you but it also insulates you against failure. How I judged myself on that first attempt was this: if I got to High Camp—26,200 feet, higher than I'd ever been—I could come home feeling successful. In hindsight, that was a mistake.

I heard about the 1963 American expedition. All the members were qualifying their chances for success: "If we get a good weather window...", "If we stay healthy...", "We're going to give it a good shot." But Jim Whitaker spoke confidently, "I'm going to the top." He started seeing it and visualizing it. I visualized it occasionally, yet, in my heart of hearts I didn't really believe I was ready, that I would be strong enough to stand on the summit.

It was a slippery slope. On the one hand, you wanted to say, "I can do this." On the other, you didn't want to be thinking "summit at all costs". So much of a mountaineer's perception of success was based on the summit. That's the measurement. A good trip is a safe trip with lots of great camaraderie. But we wouldn't be doing this if we didn't want to get to the top—that's the cherry on the sundae. The sundae is pretty good, but it's the cherry that makes it. We have big egos, too. We don't want people to think of us as failures. But I don't think I was audacious and secure and confident and cocky enough—I would never tell anyone, "I'm going to the top."

TEARS AT THE AIRPORT

You don't sleep the night before a trip like Everest. You're thinking so many stupid things, "When do we leave for the airport? I don't want to go too early and have to sit there all day, but I don't want to be late?" You're wondering if you forgot to pack something.

During one of my gear sorts the week leading up to the start of the trip I was watching the movie, *Vertical Limit*. It's such a crappy, lousy movie it's laughable. It was supposed to be this serious drama, but for me it was a full-on comedy. I noted as I was packing that I'd forgotten the nitro, which is what they all carry up K2. How else would you dislodge someone from a crevasse?

I remember it being very somber at the airport. Waiting and waiting. Maggie was just great. My climbing buddy

Gary Fallesen stopped by to give me a book, Pat Ament's *Climbing Everest: A Meditation on Mountaineering and the Spirit of Adventure*, which I read on the flights over. Then he left Maggie and me alone. When it was time to go, I told her I'd miss her and we had a nice kiss—probably the last one for about three months. Then she looked at me and burst out crying. Her weeping face reminded me of the importance of returning home safely. It also reminded me how selfish we are as climbers, leaving loved ones behind.

When I looked back from the security gate, Maggie was standing there in tears. I'm thinking, "She's got to drive home alone. What a jerk you are." It was tough because I knew I had to turn my back on that part of my world and focus on what needed to be done.

The first leg of my trip was Rochester to Pittsburgh. The passenger next to me said, "You going to Pittsburgh?" Well, no. I'm going to Pittsburgh and then to L.A. and eventually to Kathmandu.

I stayed overnight in Los Angeles, where most of the team was meeting for the overseas flight. When I checked into the hotel the bellhop looked at my two duffels and said, "Going on a little trip?" Yeah, 10 or 12 weeks. Just to Everest.

When you'd tell people where you were going they either thought it was the coolest thing in the world or that you were the biggest dope on the planet. There's not a lot of in between when it comes to something like this.

In L.A. I called Maggie a bunch of times. She said she was fine after crying at the airport, that she didn't cry all the way home. She said she'd be fine, which I knew wasn't completely true.

The next day, I went to LAX early. What else was I going

to do, visit the Hollywood Walk of Fame? Even though the hotel was at the airport, I thought there might be some traffic. OK, there wasn't. I looked around for people who looked like they might be going on a climbing expedition. I found them. There were about 40 duffels sitting on the floor. This guy, Mark Tucker, Eric Simonson's assistant, was organizing the duffels. I went up to him, introduced myself and offered to give him a hand. He accepted. Then he laughed and said, "Don't think this means you're not going to have to carry your load when you get there."

Everyone was wandering around, zombie-like, the way you do at the start of a big trip. We were all wondering, "What awaits us?" What awaited us first was a long flight from L.A. to Bangkok. We had plenty of company, too. There were three expeditions on that plane. Pete Athans was going back to Everest and Rob Link was taking a team to Dhaulagiri. Now it was getting exciting. I was surrounded by a bunch of mountaineers. Phil Ershler was a legend. Athans was a legend. I was starting to feel like Wayne and Garth in *Wayne's World*—"I'm not worthy." I felt like the least competent and accomplished climber on the plane. It really was going to be a long flight.

K-K-K-KATHMANDU

Rob Link was a guide Gary Smith and I met on Aconcagua in 1995. He'd bought some duty-free Scotch in Bangkok and apparently drank some of it before sitting down next to me on the plane. He was a little blurry-eyed. I wasn't drinking because I was Mr. Serious—and I was freaking out. But he gave me some good advice. He told me, "Don't bust your ass until you get above Camp 3. That's when you get serious. Be patient until that point and then be tough." We talked about pressure breathing and a bunch of other things. He told me, "If it's warm when you make the move from Camp 3 to Camp 4, have a Sherpa bring your down suit up." My head was swimming. I was already on sensory overload. I remember I really enjoyed talking with him. Turns out, all of what he said was true. Not that I followed his advice. Then I looked out the window at the countryside. Oh my God, we were coming into K-K-K-Kathmandu.

Kathmandu was a long way from Rochester, N.Y. It was the afternoon of March 23. I had been on the go for four days, and we were just arriving.

It was a huge Charlie Foxtrot when we got into the airport with all the gear coming off planes into this little terminal. One of your greatest fears was getting where you were going and then one or both of your duffels doesn't arrive. You're sleep-deprived from two and a half days of flying and then you're waiting impatiently to make sure your gear has made it.

One of the things Simo told us was, "Take a big, deep breath. You're not in the U.S. any more. Things are s-l-o-w-e-r. They'll get it done, eventually." Both of my duffels showed up, eventually.

Kathmandu was smoggy and badly littered. I imagined the hygiene was horrific. There were so many sights and sounds and, of course, smells. There was also all the traffic to watch out for—cars, bikes, buses, rickshaws, people, and an occasional cow—all jammed into streets that were too narrow. Everyone was driving like a maniac, missing pedestrians and cars by the slimmest of margins. In Katmandu, it was heads up all the time.

Being in a strange city I was a bit leery about walking around on my own and had trepidations over all of the Maoist activities—so I hung around the hotel. We all met for dinner at 7 p.m. in the hotel. It was awesome Tibetan cuisine—Mo Mos, a flaming pot of various vegetables, seafood and meat, plus a wonderful soup. Tomato, I think. But unlike anything I'd had before.

I wasn't really interested in sightseeing. Just looking forward to getting to Lukla and making it to the relative safety of Base Camp. Plus, I had a preconceived negative image of Kathmandu. But after a good night's sleep, I hit the town with some of the guys in the trekking party. We went to the Monkey Temple and Durbar Square. This 13-year-old kid glommed on to us and became our tour guide. People everywhere wanted to sell you something, which isn't a big deal; you just smiled and said, "No thanks." Except for Nate, one of the trekkers, who was kind of a hippie throwback from the '60s. He was such a sweet soul, he talked to everyone. Soon he was the Pied Piper of Kathmandu. Some Maharishi type came up to him and dropped flower petals into his hair and rubbed a red dot onto his forehead, and then Nate gave him a couple of rupees. I politely declined.

It was cool to be in Kathmandu, yet I was anxious about getting going. This wasn't why I was here. I was here for Everest. I wanted to get to the mountain.

NEPAL'S MOUNTAIN OF SORROW

Since 1996, there'd been a Maoist insurgency in Nepal. The country was desperately poor. The western part of the country has extremely bad land for farming. There were pockets of discontent throughout the country. The Maoists started uprising, claiming government corruption. In June, 2001, Crown Prince Dipendra massacred most of the royal family, including King Birendra. Trouble heated up. The U.S. State Department warned against unnecessary travel into Nepal. Of course, I considered my travel necessary. You put so much mental, physical and emotional commitment into a climb like this, you didn't want to pull the plug on it. No Westerners had been affected by the uprising so I just continued training, although with this little black cloud hanging over the trip.

One Sunday I saw a news crawl on the TV screen reporting that Maoists had overrun a Nepalese police station. There were 450 dead. Four hundred and fifty dead! A major deal. But our trip was still on. There was enough danger on the mountain. But now I was thinking, "Is a Maoist going to stick a gun in my face?" At one point, they closed the airport in Lukla. Apparently some Maoists had exploded a couple of bombs at the airport. IMG contacted us and told us to bring some extra money in case we needed to hire helicopters to fly us in. The trip was cloaked in stuff like that, even when we arrived.

After getting to the hotel in Kathmandu, Simo summoned us together and went over a few logistics. One of these was kind of disturbing. The State Department had just issued a warning to U.S. citizens traveling in Nepal. The Maoist had called for a *bandh* (a general strike). The State Department also said some tourist areas might be targeted and could be caught in the crossfire.

In my journal I wrote:

I think we'll be fine once we're headed toward base camp, but right now it's a bit disconcerting.

After that cheerful briefing, Ted Wheeler, (another non-guided climber on the trip) and I had a quick bite at the Radisson across the street. We got to bed early since we had a 4:30 a.m. wake-up call, breakfast at 4:45, and a 5:15 departure to the airport. However, I barely slept a wink. My mind was a whirlwind of racing thoughts about Maoists, my mental toughness, my physical toughness, etc., etc. I maybe slept one hour. Oh, well, things will adjust.

To me, the Maoist problem was an inconvenience that could ruin my plans. We mountaineers tend to be a selfish lot, thinking mostly of ourselves. But to the people of Nepal, it is a tragedy with no end in sight. To date, over 11,000 people have lost their lives. Hundreds of thousands more have been injured and displaced. Tourism, and its much-needed dollars, have all but dried up. The mountain of sorrow that rises above Nepal is much taller than Everest. I hope and pray the people of Nepal find a quick and peaceful solution to their ongoing unrest.

HEADING TO BASE CAMP AND THE DEAD YAK IN ROOM 5

The flight from Kathmandu to Lukla was short, less than an hour, and ended abruptly. We made the trip in a twin-engine plane operated by Yeti Airlines. The plane could make short approaches and takeoffs, which was essential because Lukla Airport has the shortest paved strip that provides commercial air service in the world.

Balancing the load is important on all planes, but here it was especially vital. So at Tribhuvan Airport in Kathmandu, they carefully weighed all the bags, all our duffels and the duffels of the other expeditions. Amazingly, we still got off the ground pretty much on time.

The elevation of Kathmandu is 4,593 feet and as you take off you immediately see the hills starting to rise up below you. It was terraced farmland. There weren't many roads. The hills kept climbing and climbing. You flew over a pass and you were only about 1,200 feet above the ground, yet you're flying at 11,000 or 12,000 feet. Up and up we went, then we heard the engine whining and began this steep approach into Lukla. There was a cliff-like formation just before the approach end of the runway and then, at the other end, the beginning of a steep mountain. As we touched down, we came screaming toward the end of the runway—a wall of rock coming closer and closer, and then a quick turn onto the parking tarmac. It was amazing. The approach and landing were spectacular. I decided it was not an approach I would want to do, as a pilot, without someone sitting next to me who knew what they were doing.

When we landed, everyone was psyched. Our spirits high. All the talk of the airport possibly being closed because of the Maoists could be forgotten. Everyone's bags arrived. We were set to begin a 12-day trek to Base Camp. At long last I felt like the Maoist problem was behind us. Now I could do what I came to do. I could enjoy the hike and the beautiful countryside. It was incredible. It started out pretty great—and was getting better.

We were a big group because the climbing party and trekking group were hiking in together. The climbing party consisted of:

Eric Simonson, the expedition's overall leader.

Mark Tucker, a Himalayan veteran who had summitted Everest and who also had led many climbs on Denali, Aconcagua, and in Bolivia. He was Simo's assistant, referred to as the "service provider."

Ang Passang Sherpa, the leader, also known as the Sirdar of our all-star Sherpa team that included fifteen climbing

Sherpas and six camp staffers, among them the ever-smiling Pemba Sherpa, our head cook.

Dr. Lee Meyers, our expedition physician.

Phil and Susan Ershler, Ted Wheeler, Stuart Smith and me, the non-guided climbers.

Of course, Phil and Susan were attempting to become the first husband-wife duo to climb the Seven Summits. Ted was from Portland, Oregon. The year before, he'd climbed to near 25,000 feet from the North Side of Everest with IMG. He'd retired at thirty-five (my hero). He was also an instrument-rated private pilot. Stuart, an attorney from Waco, Texas, had climbed two 8,000-meter peaks—26,906-foot Cho Oyu and 26,360-foot Gasherbrum II. He did G2 without supplemental oxygen. And he was also a pilot.

Compared to my paltry experience, everyone in the party had accomplished great things. Again, with this group I was feeling like the schmoe.

From Lukla, at 9,186 feet, it was thirty-five miles to Everest Base Camp, at around 17,500 feet. You went slowly, to acclimatize. Lukla had an airport, but no roads. There were trails. Everyone walked. There were no motor vehicles, not even motorcycles or scooters.

The first few steps on any journey, it was like, "Wow. Gosh, we've got a long way to go." It's exciting. Especially when you were out in the countryside and had no idea what was around the next corner.

We stopped in Namche Bazaar, a very colorful village carved out of the side of a mountain. There were about 1,000 residents living in dwellings with blue roofs. This was the Sherpa capital. Sherpa is a race of people; it is not a job description. Westerners often don't realize this. Sherpas are a super strong people originally from Tibet who have lived forever at high elevations. Their hearts and lungs are bigger. They are a very gentle, friendly people who believe in Buddhism. Some of the most wonderful people I've met are Sherpas. They are small in stature, but big in heart—both literally and figuratively. The climbing Sherpas are superstars in their country. But they don't climb for fun; what they do is a good paying job in a poor country.

From Namche Bazaar we made our way to the town of Na. It was a joke to call it a town since it consisted of two teahouses. Teahouses were set up all along the trekking routes. Tourism was a big deal to this country. You could get a room for less than $1 a night. There were stores that sold chocolate and water. You bought bottled water every day. You didn't trust the water quality in the streams. The stores also sold Coke, beer, and Everest whiskey. We didn't stay in the teahouses. We would set up our tents near them. Actually, the porters set up our tents for us. They would also bring us bed tea and warm water to wash with in the morning when we woke up.

At Na, we were playing Nerf football. Mark Tucker, who's like a 44-year-old camp counselor, got us playing a game. Of course, it was uneven terrain and I thought, "This would be a nice way to end a trip, turning an ankle playing Nerf football on the way to Base Camp." It was then that we learned that there was a dead yak in Room 5 in the teahouse. We weren't sure why it was there. We never found out. All we know is they pulled the dead yak out of Room 5 and dumped it in the stream, which again makes you suspect of the drinking water.

I'M NOT GOING TO MAKE IT TO
BASE CAMP

On the fifth day of the trek I came down with a case of gastrointestinal malaise. In other words, the shits. Up until then, I'd been doing fine. I'd been making my regular visit to the "little blue tent" (the bathroom). Then, all of a sudden, I was going every one and one half hours. When you're climbing, you tend to experience this sort of thing at some point during most every climb, but this was as bad as I'd ever had it.

I decided to go see Dr. Lee Meyers, our expedition physician. He'd been the doc on Simonson's Mallory expedition, and was pretty hardened. If something's not broken or falling off, he didn't get too concerned. He told me I'd live.

The group was supposed to climb 17,550-foot Gokyo

Ri for what was said to be a spectacular view of Cho Oyu, Everest, Lhotse, Makalu and Cholatse. Not me. I was eating Imodium.

After leaving Namche, you get your first view of Everest. It's 20 miles away as the crow flies. But the first time you see it, it's pretty intimidating. It looked kind of steep, with a plume of snow coming off the summit. Another one of those times when you think, "What am I doing here?" I felt the same about McKinley, even Rainier. They always seemed impossibly high.

When we got to Phortse, I was spending more time in the blue tent than in my own tent. My outlook on life was awful. I started thinking, "I'm not even going to make it to Base Camp." We'd only made it to 14,500 feet. We were not even half as high as Everest, and I was turning to mush. I had another terrible night and decided I had to go see Dr. Lee again. "Unless you're gushing blood," he said, "don't worry about it." He gave me Cipro, an antibiotic. It saved my ass, literally.

At Phortse, we got to visit the home of one of the Sherpa's parents. They gave us a kata, a friendship scarf. We drank Sherpa tea. I still wasn't feeling well, but it was wonderful to be in their home and to see how happy they were to have us as their guests. The parents were very proud of their son, who was a high-altitude Sherpa. That's a big deal.

Our next stop was in Dingboche. I learned here that Simo had told Stuart to keep an eye on me. When I heard this, I was a little mad. Not at Eric or Stuart, but at myself. I thought, "Oh, my gosh, now I'm a lowly trekker who can't even make it to Base Camp." I was feeling pretty pitiful. But in Dingboche, all of a sudden, the Cipro kicked in. It was like a light switch was flipped. I was able to eat for the first time in 36 hours. I had a Coke, which tasted so great I couldn't believe it. I ate a Hershey bar with almonds. Yum. It felt so good to feel good again.

All along the way, this self-doubt kept creeping in, "You're not good enough. Everyone else is better than you. You're not going to make it. Why are you here?" As we pushed further toward Base Camp, between Tuglha and Lobuche, there were all these chortans on the hill. Chortans are rock memorials for fallen mountaineers, most of them being Sherpas who had died while climbing. Fifty or sixty of them shrouded in clouds, gave you a reverential feeling— another reminder of what can go wrong on Everest.

The last village on the trek was Gorak Shep. Gorak is a raven-like bird and shep means dead. I could relate to shep. Kala Patar, a trekking peak, sat next to Gorak Shep. Most trekkers climbed it for the glorious views it offered of Everest. The peak was only 18,400 feet high. No big deal, really.

From Kala Patar, you headed for Everest Base Camp, which was to be our home for God knows how long.

Base Camp was at the foot of the Khumbu Glacier, and it was like camping on a rock quarry. It was a jumbled mess of rocks and boulders all over the place. As spring wears on at Base Camp, you hear water running underneath the rocks beneath you during the afternoon. We were each assigned our own tent, which was very important. You spend 45 days at Base Camp or above it. It's good to have some of your own space. Much of the time you just lay around listening to music. The iPod was the best piece of equipment I took to Everest. Right out the door of my tent, you could see up the Khumbu Icefall, with Nuptse to the right and the west shoulder of Everest to the left.

We shared a community mess tent. They brought in a heater. All of the comforts of home.

On a typical day, the temperature at night was below freezing. But as soon as the sun hit the tent, about 7:15 or 7:30 a.m., it turned nice and warm. Breakfast was at eight, lunch at noon, tea at three. In the afternoon, the clouds rolled in and it snowed. The afternoon tea was another excuse to drink and eat. Part of the deal at cushy Everest Base Camp was to eat and drink as much as you could. That's because you go to Everest in the best shape of your life, but you can't keep weight on once you're there. The irony is that when you need to be your strongest, on summit day, that's probably when you're at your weakest.

The Sherpa cook tent was made of stones. Sherpas had their own tents. There was a communications tent, where the satellite phone was kept. I'd use that to call Maggie at home every week or so. There was also a supply tent with all of our oxygen bottles and other equipment. It was like living in your own community. All around Base Camp there were these other little communities, maybe 10 or 12 expeditions from all over the world.

After we arrived, they wanted to check everyone's oxygen (O_2) saturation. I hated doing that. I'm always lower than everyone else. "Why can't I be perfect?" Normally, when red blood cells pass through the lungs, 95 to 100 percent of them are loaded (or saturated) with oxygen to carry through your arteries to all of your internal organs. At higher elevations, this becomes problematic. Your O_2 saturation decreases. One of the women in the trekking group doing Island Peak, who had never been at altitude, had an O_2 sat of 85 percent.

Great! Mine was 69, which stinks. If you were at sea level with a 69, they'd rush you to the hospital. On Denali in 1992, at 17,320 feet I'd had a weird bout of altitude sickness. That's always in the back of your mind when you go high. "Will it happen again? Was I going to be able to acclimatize properly?" Tracy, the woman with no mountain-climbing experience, was 85 and I was a lowly 69.

"Oh, well," I thought, "breathe, drink water and eat. At least I'd made it to Base Camp."

A KHUMBU WAKE-UP CALL

The climb of Everest began in earnest with a ceremony known as the puja. You brought boots, ice axes, crampons— all the important stuff—to be blessed by a Buddhist monk who had hiked up for the occasion. The puja (pronounced "poo-ja") was very important to the Sherpas to start the expedition. It was important to have a good puja. We were guests in their country and so we took this seriously. I thought it an honor to be involved in something so significant. It was plenty cold out on the morning of April 5, but I forgot the numbness in my toes as I marveled at the wonderment of the scene. The puja began with the monk and one of our Sherpas sitting in front of a stone altar that was built for the occasion. It started somberly, with chanting and the reading of scripture. Juniper was burned. The monk threw rice. We were all given some rice. As it went on, there was more chanting and we were all throwing rice on cue from our monk. It got to be more fun and festive at it went along. They smeared tsompa, a type of barley flour, on everyone's faces. We drank Chang, the local beer, which actually was quite hideous tasting. At the end of the ceremony, it was all very jovial. The wooden puja pole was erected within the center of the altar. The pole was secured and colorful prayer flags were strung in six or eight directions. Everyone was cheering and happy. It was a magical moment and I was profoundly happy as I drank it all in. Well, almost all of it. I passed on the Chang.

When the puja ended, the trekkers left. It was time to climb the mountain.

In my journal on April 6, 2002, I wrote:

The icefall should be fixed by the end of tomorrow. I hope I'm up to the task. From my tent I have a perfect view up the icefall. Wow! I think I'm the least experienced member of this team, but I'll just have to take it day to day. My next goal is to climb the icefall and spend a night at Camp 1 and then descend back to BC the next day.

The first barrier was literally at the doorstep to Base Camp (BC). It was only a ten- or fifteen-minute walk to the start of the Khumbu Icefall. It's fair to say that the Icefall had been on the climbers' minds from the beginning. It was famous—justifiably so. During the trek to BC, we discussed the ladders. I admitted that I tried to train for the ladder crossings back home. To "train," I'd put on my double-plastic boots and crampons, lay an aluminum ladder across some cinder blocks in my garage and then tried to cross without losing my balance. I failed consistently. Not quite the confidence-building exercise I had hoped for. I was only slightly consoled to learn that Stuart and Ted also tried to train back home, with the same results.

On April 9, we decided to take a little shakedown hike part way up the icefall. We wanted to gain some real experience in crossing ladders and ascending the fixed lines. Fortunately, Phil and Susan Ershler joined us. They were technically non-guided clients, like Ted, Stuart and me. However, Phil essentially guided us. He was awesome, one of the best in the business and yet he cheerfully helped us. Before we reached the first ladder, we confessed to Phil about our less-than-stellar ladder-training experiences back home. He kind of chuckled and explained that the ladders used in the Icefall are of the attic variety. The space between the rungs is narrower, so it was a little more secure, a little easier. That was all well and good but when three, four or five of these ladders are lashed together, it still got pretty bouncy. You had to be especially careful.

On our first foray above Base Camp, we went about one-third of the way up the Icefall. We took lots of photos enroute because the scenery was amazing. We discussed the objective dangers with Ersh. The ladders over the crevasses were scary, but what you learned to respect and fear were those huge, honking, hanging seracs that were as big as a garage. Seracs are blocks of ice that are formed where the glacier surface is fractured. The Khumbu Icefall is filled with thousands of seracs. And they were going to shift and fall—eventually. You just hoped it wouldn't be on you.

We asked Phil, "Hey, Ersh, should we wear our helmets through the Icefall?"

"Doesn't matter," he said. "The kind of ice that's going to

hit you there is going to crush you and your brain bucket."

Of course, as we were carefully crossing over the ladders, the Sherpas just came bouncing along. They crossed about four times faster than us—smiling and talking the whole way.

We decided our first trip into the Icefall—even though it was only the first third—was a success. A bit scary, but not as hard as I thought it would be. It was breathtaking both in terms of beauty and in lack of oxygen. Soon, we'd be climbing all the way through the Icefall and above.

The first time through the entire Icefall for Ted, Stuart and me took place on April 11. (Phil had developed a cough and he and Susan decided to wait a few days before heading up.) I found that day to be particularly difficult. We hit the Icefall at about 6 a.m. I was a little behind. I rushed to get my gear on and then I chased after Ted and Stuart as fast as I could. But I wasn't fast enough. So I finally said screw it and climbed at my own pace. The route was entirely fixed so it didn't really matter.

The first forty-five minutes in the Icefall you don't even hit a ladder. Then it gets more technical. Even though I had been in Base Camp about a week, I was still not that well acclimatized. There was also the fear of the unknown. I was nervous about that. Everyone had heard the stories of people dying in the Icefall. It wasn't something I thought about every step of the way, but there were times when you looked up and saw a serac hanging there. You tried to move fast. But above 18,000 feet that's not something that happened easily.

I made good time up the first half, but on the last half I was agonizingly slow. It was pretty high altitude and I just couldn't catch my breath. I finally emerged from the Icefall at about noon. Six hours. I was told that the next time through would be quicker. But I was still down on myself; I thought I sucked.

At the top of the Icefall, the route turns left and ascends and descends over rolling terrain. There were some monster crevasses. It was wicked hot and I made slow, but steady progress up to Camp 1. I was panting, trying to breathe, trying to protect myself from getting super sunburned while taking off some layers. I arrived at 1:15 p.m. I was gassed, totally spent. It was bad. But, on the other hand, we were at 20,000 feet—almost as high as Denali.

We spent the night there. This was the highest I'd ever slept, and it worried me. I had a bit of a headache. So much of the energy you use is wasted worrying about things you can't do anything about. Originally we'd planned on climbing up the Icefall and then back to Base Camp on the same day. However, after talking acclimatization strategy with Simo, we decided to spend two nights at Camp 1 followed by a couple of nights at Camp 2. That was more aggressive than most, but Simo reasoned it would help us get better acclimated—if our bodies could handle it.

In my journal on April 12, I wrote:

Rest day. Ted promotes the idea of an acclimatization hike up toward Camp 2. Just an hour up and an hour back. I'm pretty gassed almost immediately. Yesterday's big climb and the altitude leave me moving in slow motion. Fortunately Stuart feels the same way and he suggests we turn around after half an hour. We arrive back in time for lunch —cheese, tuna, peanuts and a beef stick. After a couple rounds of hot drinks we retreat back to our tents to relax. Tomorrow we're supposed to go to Camp 2 and spend two nights. This may

be too fast for me so I will wait and see how I feel in the a.m.
I may go down tomorrow and rest up for the next trip up.
Camp 2 is at 21,300 feet or so. We'll see.

On April 13, we hiked up from Camp 1 to Camp 2.
There were a bunch of crevasses, some ladders and even
some rappel sections at the beginning. After that, it was just
a slow plod up the Western Cwm (pronounced coom), which
extends about two miles (a cwm is a steep-walled semicircular
basin). It could be exceptionally hot, like being a bug under
a magnifying lens with the sun beating down on you.

People always asked, "How cold is it on Everest?"
That's a fair question. It's hypothermic cold. But there are
times when it's so hot you sunburn your tongue because it's
hanging out of your mouth while you're gasping for air.

After a while, Ted and Stuart were about twenty-five
minutes ahead of me, so again I ended up going alone. If
you're roped up, you arrive together. This was different. You
seem to accept a little higher level of exposure here. Between
Camp 1 and Camp 2, and from Camp 2 to the bergshrund
beneath the Lhotse Face, there were some exposed areas (a
bergschrund is a large crevasse that separates flowing ice from
stagnant ice at the head of a glacier). If I had to do it again,
I wouldn't hike there without being roped up. You aren't in
the Icefall, but you're on a glacier and there are hidden traps
all around.

The route steepened a bit as we went up the final section
towards Camp 2, located at the upper end of the Western
Cwm. To make matters worse, it took me almost forty-five
minutes to go from the first tent you see when you reach
Camp 2 up to IMG's Camp. It was only four hundred to five

hundred yards, but it took that long. It was torture. We were the last fucking tents on the left. It seemed like forever to get to them.

Camp 2 is also known as Advanced Base Camp (ABC). It was an excellent elevation to stay at to get acclimatized. Life there was fairly easy. We had two big dome tents set up for us to eat in and two cooking Sherpas who prepared our meals. Plus, we had another six or eight sleeping and storage tents. But I spent two miserable nights. I was alone in my tent, thinking we were going too fast. A lot of times people would climb to the top of the Icefall the first time and turn back. Not us. We were sleeping above 21,000 feet.

I woke up with a major, pounding headache. I tried to read a book, but I was so uncomfortable and there was that fear of the unknown again. "What was this going to turn into?" I was in my tent thinking, "I got my butt kicked in the Icefall. I was slow. I sucked there. I had a headache at Camp 1 and now a monster pounder at Camp 2. Maybe this is my personal boundary." Simo and others were saying I was going to feel better the next time. But it lingered in the back of my mind. "This was only Camp 2. What was going to happen at Camp 3 or 4?"

A CAMP 3 WAKE-UP CALL

It is infinitely easier going down. Stuart and I left Camp 2 at 7:10 a.m. on April 15 to return to Base Camp. (Ted opted to stay another night at Camp 2.) We ran into Phil and Sue Ershler at Camp 1 and exchanged pleasantries. Then we descended through the Icefall. I felt great and made good time. I actually beat Stuart down.

It was hot descending through the Icefall and a section of the route had been destroyed by a falling serac. No big deal, we just skirted around it to the right. It would have been deadly, though, if you were there at the wrong time. We reached Base Camp a little before noon. Just in time for lunch.

We spent almost a week in Base Camp. R&R. Then, on April 21, it was time for Ted, Stuart and me to head back up.

This foray would take us to Camp 3. We planned to spend one night there without supplemental oxygen. Little did we know what awaited.

The second trip to Camp 1 was better. I made good time—4 hours, 15 minutes. I was still the last one, but it was a little more respectable. We spent one night there. No headaches. Then up to Camp 2. I was feeling pretty good at this point. I was thinking, "OK, that little mountain is hurdled."

It was my 45th birthday when we climbed up to Camp 2. The year before I'd spent my birthday with Maggie in France. April in Paris. We celebrated at La Focquettes—a fancy restaurant on the Champs d' Elysee—a great time and a great meal. Now my waiter was Mingma Sherpa.

In my journal on April 22, I wrote:

I'm extra homesick on my birthday. I wish I were spending it with Maggie. Ah, the yin and yang of Everest. On one hand I want to get a shot at the summit and on the other hand I want my cushy life back! It's 5:30 p.m. now and it's gently snowing. I'm about to slip into my down suit and head to the cooking tent. Can't wait to be in Maggie's arms. But when?

We rested at Camp 2 on April 23 and on the 24th we ventured out onto the Lhotse Face. It was spectacular. There are fixed lines and it's quite steep. The face is about 4,000 feet, stretching from 22,000 to 26,000 feet. It reminded me of the fixed ropes on the Denali Headwall, but we climbed up to 22,400 feet—2,000 feet higher than Denali. I was closing in on a personal altitude record, where every step would be a new all-time high.

On April 25, we rested again. We heard that winds were supposed to come up in the evening so we shored up our tents. As promised, the wind arrived and it was fairly blustery. On the morning of the 26th, we delayed our departure to Camp 3 because of the wind. But then we saw a bunch of Sherpas going up so we took off at about 7:45 a.m. As we headed up the Western Cwm toward the Lhotse Face, the wind picked up in intensity. Before too long, all of the Sherpas had turned around and headed back to Camp 2. If those studs spun, I knew we would, too. So, within an hour of taking off, we were back at Camp 2.

After eating some breakfast in the mess tent, I retreated to my personal tent. That's when the wind started to really increase, and before long we were in the throes of a full-blown windstorm. It was probably gusting to 70 or 80 mph. The main cooking/eating tent got shredded. We all tried to brace our individual tents, which was no easy task with the wind whipping granular snow that really stung our faces. We were in survival mode, at least so far as the camp was concerned.

Ershler, who was with us now at Camp 2, told us to relax. "I've never abandoned a camp yet," he said. "We're going to save this."

It was hard, exhausting work from 11 a.m. until 4:30 p.m. Especially since we were at 21,300 feet. We finally secured the campsite as best we could and had dinner at 6:30 p.m. We returned to our individual tents at about 7:30 and the wind mercifully abated, but only for about 30 minutes. Then it was back to ripping. Not quite as bad as in the afternoon, but still bad. I sat up in the tent in my down suit with everything packed in case the tent came apart. It sounded like gravel hitting the sides, sandblasting the tent. It was dark, except for little sparks from static electricity flying off the nylon. It was pretty weird. Then, finally, at about 2 a.m., the wind stopped.

We were quite haggard from the windstorm, so April 27th turned into another rest day.

From ABC to Camp 3, you had to ascend the final slopes of the Western Cwm to get to the base of the Lhotse Face. It took us one and one half hours and that got us to about 22,000 feet. Then it was 2,000 feet up the steep Lhotse Face to Camp 3. The route was entirely fixed with ropes attached to anchors that use either pickets or ice screws. To ascend, one used an ascender that slides up the fixed ropes, but doesn't slide back. I had practiced this technique with Craig John in New Hampshire. It took us about four and one half hours to go up to the Lhotse Face to Camp 3. Exhausting—steep, thin air and moderate ice climbing.

We got to Camp 3 about 1:30 or so. Camp 3 was a desperate perch in the ice. Tent platforms had been chopped into the steep ice in a terrace-like system. Safety lines were strung from tent to tent. People had gone out to go to the bathroom without being clipped into the ropes or without their crampons and had taken the big fatal slide. There was no margin for error here. You sleepwalk; you're a dead person.

Just before we got to Camp 3 the wind had picked up. Just enough to make our grim perch even grimmer. Ted and I shared a tent while Stuart got his own. The tents were so small they felt claustrophobic. But they were nearly bomb proof against the wind. Still, it was almost impossible to sleep because of the lack of oxygen and space. Plus, the roaring winds kept the tents flapping noisily all night. I longed for the light of morning so we could get the hell back to Camp 2—or lower. But when the morning of April 29 dawned, the storm, if anything, was stronger.

Wait it out or try to descend the fixed lines in the gale? A very difficult decision. We were getting conflicting viewpoints from ABC and BC, but in the final analysis we owned the decision. I pushed Ted and Stuart to go down because I had a bit of a headache and I was concerned that we—or, to be honest, I—might get sick as time wore on. So, at 2:45 p.m. the three of us put on our gear and headed out into the storm. The visibility opened up for a moment, but quickly closed again. It was a desperate situation at best. Ted and I started down with Stuart right behind us—or so we thought. Ted and I descended a few hundred vertical feet and there was still no sign of Stuart. We were in radio communication with Ershler and Mark Tucker at Advanced Base Camp and Simo at Base Camp. Stuart and I both had a radio. Ted and I didn't know where Stuart was at the time, but we were now fully committed to descending. Finally, Stuart checked in on his radio and said that his glasses fogged up and his hands got dangerously cold putting on his crampons. His crampon straps were a little short and he had to remove his gloves as he wrestled with his crampons. He'd never left Camp 3. Ershler came on the radio and said, very authoritatively, "Stuart, you stay put. Kevin and Ted, you continue down."

Descending the Lhotse Face in a blizzard was incredibly stupid. The winds were gusting to more than 50 mph and visibility was only about 20 feet. It was colder than you can imagine and managing the fixed ropes was tricky business.

Then bad got worse. We were descending and I was in the lead when, to my horror, I found the fixed line buried in the snow. We couldn't see where it came out. Ted and I tried in vain to pull the fixed lines out from under the snow and ice. To unclip and feel our way around would have been suicide. There was no visibility. One slip would have meant certain death. Ted immediately came to the unpleasant conclusion that we must re-ascend to Camp 3. The fixed lines were our "bread crumbs" back to the relative warmth and safety of our tent.

Coming down at that altitude in a blizzard had been tough, but going up was far more difficult. At that point, I started to check my watch. I figured we should be able to get back to Camp 3 by dark. But I was beginning to get more frightened. I had icicles hanging from my eyelashes, mustache and beard. It was face-numbing cold and hard to breathe. At times the gusts were so severe I had to stand with my back to the wind and wait for them to subside. And we were climbing the Lhotse Face, which was steep. At times I had to front point with my crampons to get up the steeper sections. We moved in slow motion.

We reached a section below Camp 3 where the skeletal remains of tents from years past were strewn around. A good sign, but it was still another hour or so from there back to Camp 3. At sea level it would have taken us five to ten minutes, but we were now close to 24,000 feet and it was difficult to move. At that elevation, one step is usually accompanied by four or five labored breaths. The minutes ticked away toward darkness. That was when I realized I'd only eaten a candy bar all day. Plus, I was not drinking enough water. I could understand now how people might give up in these circumstances. Not me. I was pretty sure Maggie would kill me if I quit. In moments of desperation, I focused on her face. I kept putting one foot in front of the other. We were close to our tent, sleeping bags and stove.

Ted got to the tent first and sat shivering half inside with his crampons still on. I took off my spikes and then helped Ted take off his spikes and boots. He thought his nose might be frostbitten. We were two desperate, cold men and the light was just beginning to fade.

In my journal on April 29, I wrote:

Stuart yelled something from his sealed-up tent. I think he asked us to come get the water he had warmed for us. Ted and I were busy trying to get warm so I yelled to Stuart "could you bring the water over?" He crawled out of his tent and handed us some hot water. I'm not sure he knew how desperate and uncomfortable our situation was. It turns out he made a smart decision to stay (I wish we had). Later he told us he had no idea how hammered we were. Communication at high altitude in between tents with a storm roaring is always problematic. None of us had any fun that night.

The next morning conditions were tough—it was still windy—but visibility was good and there was a better feeling in the air. Now there were only two parties at Camp 3—the three of us and two climbers from Himalayan Guides. Peter Liggett, a British climber, and his partner from the Himalayan Guides expedition pulled out of Camp 3. They knocked on our tents as they went by. "Americans, we're going down now," Liggett said. And then he was gone.

In my journal on April 30, I wrote:

I heard Eric on the radio talking about a fall on the Lhotse Face. He said there was no reason to believe it was survivable. Then he radioed me to tell of the fall. It was someone from the Himalayan Guides twosome. Eric wanted to forewarn us of what we were about to encounter. The news was surreal and I was numb from it. I knew it was a terrible tragedy, but I was tired and I had all I could do to keep it together and descend safely. Nevertheless, there was gruesome evidence of the climber's demise. There were five or six different areas where this poor soul must have bounced on the way down. Terrible images of blood and tissue stains against the white snow and blue ice.

I had to tell myself not to freak out. You could recreate and picture the fall. It had to have been violent. But you couldn't think about it. We had something to take our mind off the awful moment, though. As we climbed down the Face, Ted was quite tired. It was then and there that he was hit with a bout of diarrhea. He had trouble exposing his rear-end to the world—the bulky down suit and sit harness made access difficult. He asked me to help him, which, of course, I did. Modesty be damned. Ted kept his cool and humor in that demoralizing situation. When he was finished, we continued down the Lhotse Face. Stuart was in front of us and had to occasionally pull the fixed lines out of the snow and ice. The bloody reminders of the tragedy were ever present. With only about two hundred vertical feet left, the fixed lines again disappeared. No amount of brute force could expose them. We had to free climb down the last bit.

In my journal on April 30, I wrote:

As we got down to the base of the Lhotse Face, some members from IMG were on their way up to see if we needed any support and to tend to the grim duty of the body. Since Stuart, Ted and I were fine, albeit tired, they passed us and went to work. Dave Hahn and Ben Marshall, who were guiding for the Ford Women's Team, along with Phil Ershler, Mark Tucker, Jake Norton (women's team photographer and guide), and the deceased's climbing partner went to the bergschrund where the body ended up. They recovered his pack and some personal effects for the family and committed his body to the mountain. I understand they performed an impromptu memorial service. Outstanding behavior under a terribly difficult situation.

It had been a scary time for us. Back at ABC we were met by the Ford Women's Team that IMG was supporting, Susan Ershler, and our cooking Sherpas. They greeted us with big hugs. Our whole drama on the Lhotse Face in the storm had unfolded on the radio with everyone listening in. It had been an incredible two days. The kind of days that made you question what you were doing there. When Peter Liggett fell, I immediately thought of Maggie. I also thought about Liggett's family. Before something like that happens, those things are just statistics. You read about it, but it isn't real until it happens in front of you. There it was—right in front of me.

DEATH ON EVEREST—OUR DIRTY LITTLE SECRET (AND HOW IT COULD NEVER HAPPEN TO ME)

It could never happen to me. That's what you think. If I truly believed I was going to die climbing, I wouldn't go. When Mr. Liggett fell to his death, I had to do a lot of soul searching.

Up until that point, the closest I'd come to death on the mountain was when we were digging around for our gear cache at 19,400 feet on Aconcagua in 1995. I thought I'd found what we were looking for, but when I pulled back the tarp, I found a human hand. I could see the outline of a body under the snow. Then I noticed the ring finger on the hand that was exposed—the dead climber was wearing a wedding band. It was an extremely sobering moment.

As a mountaineer, you accept risk. You feel you can manage it. You try not to go in avalanche areas. You go in the Icefall early when it's safer. And if you're not feeling up to it, maybe you rest for another day. You always feel as though it could never happen to you. For most pilots who meet misfortune, it happens before they take off. It's the same in the mountains. It comes down to bad decision-making. Obviously, I accept a reasonable amount of risk with some of the things I do. Everyone has different levels of risk management. There are days when people climb with a lenticular cloud hanging over the mountain and you go, "Oh, my gosh, I would never do that." You think, "I'm smarter, tougher, better. Whatever." That's true and false. The bottom line is, it can happen to you. You can do everything right and still die. You have to think about death and the possibility that it might occur. But you can't dwell on it.

If a big hanging serac falls on your head in the morning, even if it's early in the morning and you're walking lightly, well, I guess your number is up. When Mr. Liggett fell I found myself asking, "Is this fair to Maggie?" I was looking at fresh blood and the reality that a party of five went up, but only four came back down alive. That was a human being, not a statistic you read on a page and dismiss.

Does the death of a climber, albeit a stranger, stop you? Obviously, it doesn't. We're selfish. But this was supposed to be fun. Even though you get your butt kicked occasionally, overall it's a joyful experience. But this cast a grim cloud over the expedition for days. It made us realize, "Yeah, it could happen to me." Then, after a little time, you collect yourself. You decide, "OK, either I'm going to go home and quit this silliness or I'm going to double my concerns and attention to safety and learn from this." That's how we took it. After a couple days of self-doubt, I reinsulated myself that it couldn't happen to me.

I went on.

Here's our dirty little secret—If no one ever died on Everest, it would not be as big a deal to climb it. If there weren't a high degree of risk involved, there would not be as high a degree of reward.

Almost anything you do that's high risk, has a high reward. And there's a fine line between success and failure. If you're an entrepreneur, the difference between doing great and not paying your bills is pretty slim. It's the same way with flying. They say that when shooting an instrument approach in the clouds, your brain is seven times more amped than a brain surgeon who is operating. But if you screw up and slam into cumulus granite, people think, "The fool." If you land without incident, people say, "Wow, what a good pilot." Same thing with climbing. People always asked, "Did you make it?" No one said, "Did you have a good time? Did you get along well? Was everyone in harmony?" It's "Did you make the summit?" The summit is invariably the measure of your success. So, obviously, we all failed quite a bit—or at least it was perceived that we failed.

You did have to accept a level of risk and understand that death could happen to you, while at the same time believing it couldn't happen to you. You appreciate life so much more once you realize how precious and precarious it is. That's one of the things you get out of climbing. You realize it could be taken away. A lot of climbing is down time. But when you are doing something, you are super dialed in. You're consumed with it.

There's a little bit of that man vs. self and man vs. nature when you climb a big mountain. I'm not sure a lot of mountaineers would say it, but putting yourself in a dangerous place excites people and they know it. Nobody goes to see a tightrope walker one foot off the ground. They want to see someone on the wire high off the ground. Maybe the thickness of the rope is the same, but it's cooler when they're higher. Why? Threat of death, I guess.

If Jon Krakauer, who is a great writer, had gone and climbed Mount Everest and nothing bad had happened, he would have written a good book. But how many millions would he have sold? When the disaster of 1996 struck Everest, the world's attention was riveted on it. *Into Thin Air* became a gigantic bestseller. Same thing with David Breashears' IMAX film. Without the tragedy it would have been an absolutely epic case of film making, but fewer people would have gone to see it. It's awful to say, but those are the facts.

Even so, while death is a part of Everest, it is not the ultimate reason why we climb it. We don't have a death wish. If I'd taken the big bivouac nap up there, then some people would have said quietly that I was a selfish jerk. Others would have said, "He died doing what he loved." That's the great write-off. You don't want to die doing what you love. You want to love what you're doing and die an old man.

When I returned to Base Camp, I called Maggie at home. In my journal on May 1, I wrote:

I was afraid she had heard of the tragedy and was freaking. I got her at work and she sounded great. She had heard about the high winds from an Internet dispatch, but not the death. As much as I tried I couldn't suppress my cough. She sounded concerned and also pointed out that it was now May 1. Her unspoken message to me was, "let's get this over with and carry on with our lives together." The message is clear, especially in light of the tragedy.

On the one hand we're really well acclimatized and we'll be ready to go after five or six days of rest. On the other hand, is it really worth it? I'm not sure, but I'm going to be extra careful and I'll turn around if it doesn't feel right.

BIG HEAD TODD, THE MONSTER

Ted's nose was not looking good. Dr. Lee said he would probably just lose some skin. But it was turning black from the frostbite. I felt terrible about it. I knew it was my fault. First of all for making him go out in the storm and then because I hadn't done anything for him when we were climbing back up the Lhotse Face. I'd seen all that ice hanging off his face, but I couldn't get to him and I couldn't communicate with him. I apologized to him in Base Camp. He said it was OK. "You had ice hanging off your face, too," he told me.

That made me feel better, especially since I hadn't gotten any frostbite from it. But it was still my dumb decision to try to go down in bad weather.

I stewed about that while I tried to rest and get healthy for our next move up the mountain. I had a nasty high-altitude cough that I couldn't shake. The Khumbu cough, as it's known, is a non-productive cough. Most people get it. Some get it so badly they'll cough hard enough to break a rib. That worried me a little.

Everyone talks about the big things that stop a climber: avalanches, falls, and cerebral or pulmonary edema. But, quite honestly, it's the little things that affect a climber's success the most. Keeping your feet blister-free, keeping ice off your extremities, keeping weight on your body. Climbing Everest is sort of like running a marathon. It's 26.2 miles and your last two or three miles don't need to be a sprint, but you need to be at your best to finish. It's a race against deterioration. The toughest day ever in the mountains is summit day. Most of your time at Base Camp is spent trying to eat, drink and be healthy—to get ready for the finish. You try to mother hen yourself. That's what I was doing.

That was when Big Head Todd reared his ugly head. Gosh, I wish I'd broken a finger—that would have been cooler. I wish I'd smacked my face on the ice and gotten a black eye, maybe even a stitch. Instead, when people asked the question, "What happened to you?" I had to say, "I have a ... hemorrhoid."

"A hemorrhoid?! Oh, aren't you the tough, little mountaineer?"

I named it Big Head Todd, the Monster because I had the song, *Resignation Superman* from Big Head Todd and the Monsters on my iPod.

I wrote in my journal on May 4:

Yesterday was miserable. It seems the center of my universe is one big fat hemorrhoid. When I move it hurts, when I cough it hurts, just about everything makes it hurt. I slept awful on the night of May 2—two or three hours of sleep. Here I am at Base Camp for R&R and I'm in constant agony. Dr. Lee gives me some topical ointments that don't seem to help.

It was disgusting. Four or five days of absolute misery. It was pitiful. It's tough to have a positive attitude and think about the summit, try to stay acclimatized and go for hikes, when your butt rules your life. I started to wonder, "Is Big Head Todd going to keep me from climbing Everest?" Imagine the sheer embarrassment of that!

You think about what could trip you up on Everest. An ice axe wound to the head would have been easier to explain. I would have rather taken 70 stitches. Instead I had days of pain and jokes pointed my way because, fortunate for me, the women's team was nearby and everyone got to talk about it. You think Reinhold Messner ever had hemorrhoids? Sir Edmund Hillary or Tenzing Norgay? Everyone laughed and thought it funny. Maybe it's funny after the fact; it wasn't funny then.

WHEN TO GO? OR, HURRY UP AND WAIT

Today is Tuesday, May 7ᵗʰ and I left Rochester 7 weeks ago! We've been on the mountain for 45 days. It seems like my life revolves around zippers. The tent, my sleeping bag, jackets, etc. I'll be happy for a scenery change.

That's what I wrote in my journal as the waiting game began at Base Camp. After spending 10 days on what we hoped would be our last acclimatization foray, we were where we wanted to be: ready to go. Now was the time to wait for a weather window to make a summit run.

At first, I didn't mind the wait. I was eager for Big Head Todd to depart, and even without hemorrhoids, you needed five to seven days to get over being so high up the mountain. I was still troubled by my Khumbu cough. But, in my head,

I knew that no one climbed Everest healthy. So I tried to stay psychologically up for the final push.

At this point we started to dream and discuss that first meal off the mountain, that first shower, and hopefully signing the wall at the Rum Doodle Bar and Restaurant in Kathmandu—a tradition successful climbers have been doing for decades. It had been a long voyage and the hardest part was right around the corner. There was a need to stay focused and motivated. That's when you have to be a bulldog.

The big buzz around Base Camp—for all the teams—was when were you going to go. On Everest in May, the jet stream moves away from the summit when the monsoon starts to move up the Indian subcontinent. It literally pushes the jet stream north and a good weather window usually opens up. To give us insight into this we received weather reports from a meteorologist in Seattle who would try to forecast the jet stream's movements. It was hoped that those forecasts would allow us the right timing to move into position high up the mountain. You need six days. You have to move from Base Camp to Camp 1, then up to Camp 2, where you spend a rest day, then to Camp 3 and finally to Camp 4. Going to Camp 2 and having bad weather is OK. You can spend some extra days at the relatively low altitude of Camp 2 with little ill effects. But if you go to Camp 3 or Camp 4 and it turns bad, you expend a lot of energy—energy that you can't afford to lose at that point.

The other factor is how far up the route the lines have been fixed. The first expeditions that move up have to do the work. So there's a bit of a waiting game with some teams saying, "No, you go first." They wait for someone else to fix the ropes.

On May 8, it appeared that Ted, Stuart, the Ershlers, Tuck and I would be moving, weather permitting, to Camp 1 the following day. In the perfect world that meant we would have a summit bid on May 14. In my journal, I wrote:

I feel like we've been running a marathon and we're at mile 21 and now it's time to sprint the rest of the way home. Just have to take it day to day and be tougher than ever on summit day. Ted, Stuart and I had a meeting with Simo, Tuck and Dave Hahn to discuss logistics from Camp 3 to 4 and then on summit day. O_2 flow rates, timing, water, clothing, etc. Basically, I think we need to reach the summit 10 hours after we depart the South Col. We'll probably leave at around 10:30 pm. So that would put us on the summit at 8:30 am. That would be too awesome!

I was nervous and excited and relieved that one way or another this expedition would be winding down.

I doubted I would have two shots at the summit. I suspected I would be too physically and emotionally drained after this push to try again late in May. But the push was put on hold the following day. On May 9, I wrote in my journal:

Ooops. Change of plans. We're going to leave tomorrow for our summit bid. Two reasons. First, the weather is supposed to be better on the 15th and 16th. But that's just a forecast. The biggest reason is to make sure the route gets fixed above the South Col. I don't think Simo wanted to wait or depend on others, so he, Phil and Tuck started to talk with other expeditions. I think we're going to work with Guy

Cotter's group from Adventure Consultants to coordinate fixing the route. Plus, Phil has solicited rope and Sherpa contributions from other teams. So it looks like we, or more appropriately our Sherpas, will lead the way.

But when? That was the question. Maybe we would leave May 10, maybe we wouldn't. It seemed like a total crapshoot to me. Six-day forecasts and waiting for the route to be fixed. Patience and flexibility must rule the day. I needed to have both.

Sometimes there's a time to go fast: you have a weather window, so let's go NOW. Other times, you just have to wait. It's the same way in business and in piloting a plane. As an entrepreneur, when you see the right opportunity you want to be there to seize it. You don't want to be impatient and grab for it at the wrong time. Pilots sometimes suffer from "get-there-itis." They takeoff when they should have stayed on the ground. Sometimes decision-making is clouded by a desire to go. You have to make sure you're mentally disciplined enough to make good decisions.

Sitting in Base Camp, we wanted to get going but didn't want to get there and have the weather suck. You just hope the weatherman gets it right and that when you get to the top the jet stream isn't going to be on the summit with you.

CAMP 3 TO CAMP 4—THE MAJOR MISCALCULATION

We started up on May 11. Finally. The plan was to climb to Camp 1 on May 11, move to Camp 2 on May 12, rest at Camp 2 on May 13, climb to Camp 3 on May 14 and go to High Camp on May 15. Then we'd get an early start for the summit, which we would hopefully reach on May 16. Then back down again. One last descent. Happily.

We ate breakfast with Simo at 4:30 a.m. on May 11. It was dark and cold. But that's the way you wanted it when you go through the Icefall. The more frozen it is, the better. After we ate, Simo had us go to the altar where the puja was held. Sherpas always burn juniper before heading up. It was supposed to bring good karma. We burned some as well. Simo took our photo and wished us well. That signaled to us that this was it. This was when it turned serious.

We would joke later that climbing Everest was pretty much an eight- or nine-day camping trip. Forget all those other weeks you put in there. It was really just this little backpacking trip in May. That's when you start breaking everything down into little pieces: just get through the day. Get to Camp 1. Feel good and take it from there. You start to think: there's only x-number of hard hours left—I can do that.

We mostly stayed together—Ted, Stuart, Phil, Sue, Tuck and me—up to Camp 1. It was uneventful. You were never totally comfortable going through the Icefall. Even though this was our seventh trip through it, it could still kill you in the blink of an eye. Besides, as it gets warmer later in the season, it falls apart.

Most groups would go from Base Camp to Camp 2. We decided not to push it. I got a good night's sleep at Camp 1, something I hadn't done the previous night in Base Camp, and the next day we moved to Camp 2. May 13 was a rest day. We sorted gear and reflected on what was happening.

Now the climbing really started. On May 14 we ascended from Advanced Base Camp at 21,300 feet up the Lhotse Face to Camp 3 at 24,000 feet. It was hot. I performed well and arrived third out of the six in our party. I'd typically always been the last one to arrive at camp. It's not a race, but you're always comparing yourself to others. So I was feeling pretty good.

At Camp 3, we slept breathing supplemental oxygen. At that point we were not worried about acclimatization; we were trying to stay healthy. The big move was the following morning—on May 15.

Rob Link, an accomplished guide and well-renowned

mountaineer, had talked to me on the flight into Kathmandu about going from Camp 3 to 4 and how you have to be a bulldog and kick it in. I wish I'd listened more carefully to him. This was where ignorance and self-doubt came into play. The plan was to get to High Camp by 1 p.m., get hydrated and by 3:30 try to get some sleep. We wanted to be ready to leave High Camp and go for the summit at 10:30 p.m. You don't want to spend too much time at Camp 4. Even sucking Os only brings you down about 3,000 feet, so your body is still deteriorating. That was why they called it the Death Zone—at this altitude; your body was slowly dying.

I never thought about the importance of going from Camp 3 to Camp 4. I thought it would be like going from Camp 2 to 3. It was only another 2,400 feet vertically. But it was the first time I'd used oxygen while climbing. The first time you strap on an oxygen mask, you feel a little bit weirded out. Within 20 steps my goggles were completely fogged and iced over. Now I was panicking. I couldn't see. You're clipping and unclipping from fixed lines as you climb, so you need to see. One missed clip combined with a slip at the wrong time would mean death. I'd seen it happen. With all you're wearing—hood, goggles, oxygen mask—you're like an astronaut. You have tunnel vision. When my goggles fogged up, I didn't even have tunnel vision. I thought, "Oh my God, I'm not even going to get out of Camp 3."

I couldn't take off the goggles. If you do that, you end up snow blind. Ershler, my hero, saw my predicament. He told me to just wipe out the goggles and relax. He said, "It'll probably resolve itself within half an hour." My visibility through the goggles improved, but it was never perfect.

Every step I took above Camp 3 was a personal high.

I was doing OK. We climbed toward the top of the Lhotse Face and then traversed diagonally in the direction of the Yellow Band at 25,000 feet. The weather, which was cold first thing in the morning, now turned hot. We were in the sun and there was no wind. I was overheating. I really needed to get out of my down suit, but when you're wearing all this astronaut stuff, how are you going to do that? It was steep, not extreme. But if you fall, you die. Tucker suggested I just unzip the top and wrap that part around my waist.

There was a bit of a back up at the Yellow Band. Many teams were moving up at the same time. We were in the commuter lane now and traffic was slowing down. As we were waiting, I was chatting with Tucker. I told him I was going to up my O_2 flow from two liters per minute to three liters per minute. The Yellow Band was kind of steep and rocky, which you're climbing over in crampons. I figured I'd need the increased oxygen flow. But Tuck asked about my oxygen reserves. My unfamiliarity with the system gave me doubts about my oxygen reserves. He encouraged me to be conservative. So I turned the flow down to 1.5 liters a minute. In hindsight, that was a huge mistake. I got really slow.

After the Yellow Band, there was another diagonal upward traverse to the Geneva Spur. About halfway into the traverse, I sat down and drank a little water. I realized I had plenty of O_2 so I bumped up my flow rate to three liters. By then, everyone in my group was well ahead of me. I felt alone. There were other people around me, from other expeditions, but with oxygen masks on it's hard to communicate. I was within myself and I was getting nervous because I was lagging behind. I was about two hours behind everyone.

The Geneva Spur was snow and rocks and a little steep

in the beginning, and toward the end of it there's a very steep section, about forty- or fifty-near-vertical feet. I climbed on four liters per minute and did pretty well, although an anchor pulled out near the top. It was backed up, but it was a scary moment. My ascender also started to ice up, which was annoying. It kept sliding back down the fixed lines.

After the Geneva Spur, it's relatively flat. A Sherpa told me it was about twenty minutes to the South Col. He was coming down and I actually asked the novice question, "How much further is it to High Camp?" It took me 40 minutes, and when I reached the Col, I was physically and emotionally spent.

I pulled in around 4 or 4:15 p.m., more than three hours behind schedule. I'd kept the walkie-talkie off, trying to conserve batteries, which was stupid. I got yelled at. I immediately declared myself out of play for a summit bid that night. I couldn't see myself being able to rest up and hydrate, go to sleep at 6 p.m. and then go do the biggest day in my life when I'd just pulled in like a dog with his tail between his legs. I was finished.

MAY 16, 2002—THE DAY I STAYED
IN THE TENT

I was just beat up. My thought was that if I could just rest for the night, breathe Os and sleep some, I'd be good for the next night. I radioed Simo. He was at best lukewarm. He was concerned about the Sherpa support. He had another team, the Ford Women's Expedition, coming along two days behind us.

I slept from 6 to 7:30 p.m. I woke up feeling much improved and even thought about calling Simo to say I was thinking about going that night versus taking my chances for support the following day. But I didn't. I wish I had. I'm sure he would have encouraged me to go. He would have told me, "Everyone feels like shit up there. You may be surprised what you can do. Go for it." Although I don't think I would have made the summit, at least I would have given it a shot.

I wish I had at least gotten out of the tent.

Instead, I helped Ted get ready. We shared a small tent at High Camp. There was no wind. It was clear. Conditions were perfect. Fucking perfect. Looking up, you could see this trail of headlamps moving up the mountain. This was the first real weather window. It was like, "Release the hounds."

The South Col was buzzing with activity as climbers and Sherpas from our team and other expeditions prepared for their pre-midnight departure. There'd been a change in the approach to the departure time for the summit. It was now much earlier and climbers hoped to summit no later than noon. The turnaround time used to be 2 p.m., but now people want to get up there by 9 or 10 a.m. That seemed a better idea since it allotted more time and daylight for descent.

After our team left, I was depressed and tormented. I put my O_2 to 1.5 liters per minute and slept quite well in my uncrowded tent until about 5 a.m. The first thing I did after waking up was turn on the walkie-talkie to listen to play-by-play and hear how everyone was doing. They all seemed to be making great progress—except for Mark Tucker, who had turned around early and was already back in High Camp. He said "the machine" just wasn't working. Tuck had summitted in 1990 from the North Side and in 2001 he turned around just before the Hillary Step on this side of the mountain. In fact, he had a T-shirt made in Kathmandu just before our trip that said, "Hillary Step, been there, didn't do that."

As I lay there, I overheard a radio call between Simo and Tucker. Simo asked Mark how I was doing. He told Eric what I'd told him—that I'd slept well and was feeling great.

"Sure, he's been sleeping on O_2 in a warm sleeping bag," Eric said, seemingly dismissing me.

"Look," I said, breaking into the radio call, "I feel strong and well and I want a shot at the summit tonight."

I was caught between the two teams. I was a logistical pain in the middle of it. Simo was very discouraging, which really pissed me off, and he told me I'd been the slowest one the entire trip. Those words really stung.

Finally he said we'd have to wait and see how our team and the Sherpas did. If everything worked like clockwork, perhaps I could go up with one or two Sherpa that evening. But it sounded like less than a 50-50 proposition.

So I laid back and listened on the radio as everything seemed to fall into place for our team. The Sherpas fixed lines on the Southeast Ridge. Everyone who was moving up, and there were probably eighty people on the route, had committed themselves to the climb with the hope that everything would work out. Simo had been on a trip where everyone got to the South Summit and no one had any more fixed line—everyone had to turn back. Part of me was thinking, "If they have to turn around, maybe that'll help my chances." That was one of those little selfish feelings you have. Then I'd catch myself: "No, no, no—these are my friends and I want them to make the summit."

Phil and Susan were ahead of Ted and Stuart. They were doing great. That's when I started thinking, "Hey, if they all summit, quickly and painlessly, and whip back down to High Camp, maybe it'll improve my chances for tomorrow."

Phil called, "Hey, Eric, guess where we are? The summit of Mount Everest. I've struggled a little today, but Susan has been an animal. Unbelievable."

The first husband and wife team to summit the highest point on seven continents. History.

Not long after that Ted reached the summit. He sounded OK. The last person to get up was Stuart. His Sherpa had asked him a couple times about turning around. He said, "No." They'd all made it—part of a record day. More than 70 climbers summitted, while I sat in the tent listening to the radio. Alone.

I was super happy for them, but I felt my chance was slowly slipping away. I felt great for them, but bad for myself. The easy and uneventful descent did not pan out. First, I heard Phil on the radio. He said, "Oh, my God." Someone had taken the oxygen bottles they'd stashed for descent. That was the first "Oh, no." Stuart passed Ted on the way down. Ted had changed oxygen bottles and masks. His goggles fogged up badly. He stopped moving for an hour on the South Summit. They started yelling at him over the walkie-talkie, telling him to get moving. Ted, calmly said, "I'll get going if everyone stops yelling at me."

The wind started to come up. The summit was no longer in view from High Camp. It was snowing a little and blowing. Not horrific, but it was unpleasant. I realized it had gone to shit for me. While I was concerned about Stuart and Ted, I felt I'd lost my shot. It was 2:30 p.m. I started sobbing in my tent. I felt so sad.

The Ershlers returned to High Camp at around 3:30 p.m. The missing Oxygen bottles were more for reserve. A little extra insurance. No harm, no foul in this case. But it could have been a big problem. Stuart came down about an hour later. Ted finally got down, just as it was getting dark, about 6 or 6:30 p.m. In my journal I wrote:

Tucker and I helped and supported the returning climbers.

I took off peoples' crampons and secured their packs, got them bottles of O2 to sleep on, etc. The wind was still blowing. I was happy for the team, but also jealous. I felt well and strong, but I knew tomorrow I'd be turning my back on the summit.

INJURY TO INSULT

Climbing back down from Camp 4 to Camp 2, I was very sad. I passed the women's team as they were moving up. I'd asked Simo if I could stay at Camp 4 and tag along with the women when they arrived. He nixed that idea because it would have meant spending three nights at the South Col, which, he felt, was an invitation to get sick and court disaster. I knew that would be his answer before I asked. Besides, it was Dave Hahn's responsibility to lead the Ford women's team, not take on another climber. And a weak one at that.

After that I couldn't turn my back fast enough on the mountain. Although I'd formulated another plan: race back to Base Camp, rest and take another shot at it. Simo would laugh that off, saying, "Man, you're really trying to make this happen. I admire your tenacity." But it wasn't going to happen.

I saw Jake Norton, who was climbing up with the women. He asked me how I was doing. I told him I was devastated.

"New PR, buddy," he said. "You should feel good about this. You have a new personal record high."

I couldn't care less about that. I was inconsolable.

I slept fitfully at Camp 2 the night of May 17. I was up just before first light, about 4:30 a.m. on May 18, and gathered my stuff. My pack was relatively heavy since I was taking everything down. It probably weighed forty-five or fifty pounds. I had some tea and a snack, and put on my crampons. I was just walking out of camp at about 5:15 a.m. when I caught a front point on my left crampon and fell hard directly on my left kneecap. I did this right in front the videographer for the women's team, Riley Morton, and our Sirdar, Ang Passang. It hurt like an SOB. Mercifully no one said, "Be careful" after the fact. I was now hurt and angry with myself for falling like a klutz. I was thinking, "This is really not needed." I started the morning in a foul mood and now I had a black cloud over my head.

Ang Passang tried to help me up, but since I was mad, I pushed him away. I was hurting emotionally and now physically. But I had no right to be so rude with Ang Passang. Later, I apologized to him for my behavior. He dismissed it. But I felt like an even bigger jerk because of the way I'd reacted. I expected my knee would be better after a little while, once I got going.

I wasn't able to walk off the knee pain. I was thinking it was going to suck going through the Icefall. As I was down-climbing, I was listening to the radio. The women's team was going for the summit and I was getting the play-by-play again. The jealous part of me was saying, "The women are going to do it." It all seemed to be happening so easily for them. Not that I'm dissing the women—they were all strong and worthy. But I was feeling sorry for myself. I was having a pity party for one.

Then everything turned to shit for them in 10 to 15 minutes. Dave Hahn made an offhanded remark, "I don't like the look of some clouds around Makalu." He was hanging back with Allison Levine. All of a sudden Allison collapsed. Hahn told Jake Norton, who was ahead of them to photograph their arrival at the summit, that he and his Sherpa needed to come back down from above the Hillary Step to help the others. Jake was just minutes away from the summit when he started down. Bad weather was coming in. Allison had dropped, and Jody Thompson and Kim Clark weren't feeling good about the situation. Jake was being ordered down, and guide Lisa Rust announced that one of her eyeballs was freezing and she was concerned about her vision. She decided it was time to come down. It was a bad scene. Then Jake was told he could go back up. Allison had responded well to increased oxygen flow and a shot of Dexamethasone. Hahn wanted Jake to get his chance at the summit. So he went back up the Hillary Step and boofed the summit. But everyone else spun. They all turned around. I couldn't believe what I was hearing.

I felt terrible for them. Plus, every step I was taking in the Western Cwm was painful, and I knew it was going to get worse in the Icefall. There are places where you have to jump over crevasses.

But I knew once I got out of the Icefall I would be safe.

I knew then that I wasn't going to die on Everest. I'd been looking forward to putting that behind me. But in my mind I was going to do it after going to the summit. I was going to live to tell the tale of standing on top of Everest. In my head. In reality, I was going to have to tell a different story.

I arrived first at Base Camp. I didn't want to get passed by anyone on my way down. I was alone with my depression. Even though I'd said on the trek into Everest Base Camp that it would be a successful trip if I made High Camp, I felt like a failure. I wanted to leave the mountain. Immediately. I wanted everything to stop hurting, including my ego.

I'M THROUGH WITH BIG MOUNTAINS
FOREVER—I'M FINALLY CURED

On May 2, before our summit attempt, I'd written in my journal:

One thing is for certain. I'll never go above 20,000 feet after this trip. Plus, I'll never be gone for this long again. EVER!

But now, as I returned to Base Camp with my tail between my legs, I was certain that was true. I wanted to get off the mountain as quickly as possible.

I was profoundly devastated. It really felt awful. Words can't describe my disappointment. Later in the day on May 18, Phil, Susan, Ted and Stuart all got down. We were going to have our last dinner together. Stuart and I had decided we were going to start the three-day trek out the next day. On the larger scale, the team had succeeded—four out of six had made it to the summit and no one was seriously injured. There was just my knee and Ted's nose, but both would heal. Somehow the Sherpas baked a cake and frosted it to look like the summit. There was a team photo, which I didn't want to be in. Well, I wanted to be in it but I didn't feel it was right. I didn't think I deserved to be in the same photo with them. There was a lot of clapping and happiness. Their success underscored my failure. I was still angry with Simo. What he said about me being the weakest member was really festering.

I gathered up my stuff. There was no joy in packing. I just wanted to get off the mountain. I woke up around 5:45 a.m. on May 19. I usually waited until the sun hit the tent, but I got up earlier. I knew Simo would be drinking coffee in the mess tent. I wanted to have a private chat. But the cooking Sherpas and Dr. Lee Meyers were there. I was feeling pretty emotional, like I could either break into tears or start yelling. I told him I felt it was unfair that he called me the weakest and always behind the rest of the team. That simply was not true. I wasn't the strongest, but I thought I mounted a credible attempt. The comments Eric made almost invalidated my time on the mountain. He apologized and told me he would rather err on the side of caution. "It's a long way up there and I wanted to make sure you got home," Simo said. "If I was harsh, I'm sorry."

I really liked Eric and when someone you respect disses you it hurts even more. Plus, I felt he was a kindred spirit. Like me, he was one of three partners in his business, and we had spent a lot of time talking about our companies and philosophies. He said he felt bad for me, but told me that I put in a good effort.

"You know, I didn't make it to the top of Everest until my third try," Simo said. "The first time, we were young and going to live forever, so I knew we'd get more chances. The second time, I was certain we'd make it, but we turned back on summit day. I was absolutely devastated. I was depressed. I understand how you feel. Failing made me want to come back and succeed."

I was thinking, "That's great for you, but I'm not coming back."

I was even angrier with myself for not giving it a shot. If only I'd tried. Intellectually, I knew why I'd done it. But in my heart I kept wondering why didn't I try to go higher. I felt better after talking to Eric—he wasn't being a jerk. I looked for someone or something to blame. But in the end it had been up to me—but now I felt almost ashamed. I never knew it would hurt that badly. I had deluded myself into believing that getting to High Camp would be respectable. It wasn't. I was done. It was time to go home. No more big mountains for me.

CHEESEDICK AT LAX—WELCOME HOME

My knee was a mess, worse than I thought when I fell on it. Even if I could have rested at Base Camp for another attempt at the summit, my knee would not have allowed it. I had a three-day walk on a sore knee. I wasn't looking forward to that.

We took photos of the six of us and it was hard to smile in those pictures. One of the nice things about the walk out was that it gave me time to decompress. I enjoyed Stuart's company on the way out. We'd sometimes been on different schedules when we were climbing, but now we walked together. Trekkers would come along and ask us how we did. When he told them he'd made the summit, I winced a little bit.

Spring was blooming and I was bumming. So much had

changed since we trekked in. There was more water flowing and flowers were out now. You could smell spring in the air—the dirt and the greenery. It was beautiful and I figured, "It must feel great to be walking out successfully, like Stuart."

The first day's trek to Pangboche was long. We reached Pheriche after six or seven hours and stopped for a Coke at a local teahouse. But the next couple of hours were painful. We arrived after dark at the teahouse where we were going to stay, the Tara Lodge. We'd been on the trail since 9:30 a.m. It cost about 45 cents for the night at the Tara Lodge. I was tired, but I woke up at 4 the next morning. We were ready to go again by 6:30 a.m.

In my journal, I wrote:

Off we go with our porters. They're smallish kids maybe 5-foot-4, 120 pounds, 16 or 17 years old. They each carry two duffels, a total weight of about 80 pounds. Incredible.

Spring was everywhere around us as we trekked. It was an odd paradox to my dark mood.

We arrived early in the afternoon in Namche, where we stayed again in the same hilltop teahouse that we stayed during our trek in. The owner was talking with Tashi, the grandson of the legendary Tenzing Norgay, the Nepalese Sherpa guide who in 1953, along with Sir Edmund Hillary, first reached the summit of Everest. We chatted them up for a while. The owner had been deaf since age 18 from meningitis but he was anxious to communicate with us. We talked and wrote down comments back and forth. I liked him very much. Another wonderful Sherpa person.

Later, Stuart and I walked down a steep hill into the

village for pizza and beer. Then I bought souvenirs from a Sherpani. She was the mother of four and very friendly. I think I was her biggest customer that day and she wanted me to have tea with her. I begged off and wandered the streets until I saw someone I met from another expedition. Just as I was saying hello, I was nearly gored by a yak that was wandering down the street. I had to grab its horn and steer it away from me. Just my luck, survive Everest but get gored by a yak!

The last day of trekking was beautiful. There was a lot of up and down, and my knee was hurting pretty bad. I was also sad as I put everything behind me. Walking out the Sagarmatha National Park gate, I remembered how happy I'd been two months earlier when we were entering. Now I was glad to be leaving.

When we returned to Lukla, I set my stuff down. I knew the major walking was done. We were staying at The Hotel Sagarmatha, the finest hotel in Lukla. The rooms cost a whopping $25 a night. Stuart negotiated them down to $15. There were sit toilets, a real shower, electric lights—I'm talking nice!

We ate near the airport. We had to negotiate to fly out. I just wanted to fly away as quickly as possible. The telephone lines to Kathmandu had been cut by the Maoists, but we got our flights straightened out. After that, we ended up in the Wave Bar, which somehow has a pool table in it. How the table got there was beyond me. All I wanted to do was drown my sorrows in as many beers as possible. I was talking to this French woman who'd made it halfway up on summit day. She was upset that she'd failed, but she was strong in her convictions that she was coming back. I admired her convictions, but I thought it was nuts. Not me. I wasn't coming back.

The next day we got on the last flight out of Lukla. It was still a spectacular flight, even in my pitiful state of mind. As soon as we reached Kathmandu, I was able to get on the plane to Bangkok. Stuart was staying overnight in Kathmandu so we said our goodbyes. From Bangkok, I'd be making the long flight back to the United States.

Before, on the flights over, everything was ready for us, we were coming together and there was this incredible promise ahead. Now I was alone, beat up, my knee was hurting, and I was leaving with an unfulfilled promise. I just wanted to get home to Maggie and have her console me.

Finally, the following morning, I reached Los Angeles. I was going through customs and there was this overweight customs officer looking at my beat-up duffels that had been living at Base Camp the last couple of months. He looked over my passport, which had a 60-day visa and an extra 10-day visa in it.

"Seventy days in Nepal," he observed. "What were you doing there so long?"

I didn't know what to say, but I had to answer.

"I was on a mountaineering expedition."

"Oh, really, where?" he asked.

"Mount Everest."

I'd dropped the E Bomb. His eyes lit up. He couldn't wait to ask me the next question.

"Did you get to the summit?"

What was I going to say? I decided to try to make myself look better. I told him I made it to 8,000 meters, to High Camp, up to the Death Zone.

"Oh, yeah?" he said, unimpressed. "How long would it have taken to get to the summit?"

"It was a day away."

"A day?" he said, incredulously. He scoffed at me. "You should have gone to the summit."

Just what I needed. Welcome back to the United States. Here was this big fat guy who probably took the escalator in the airport because the stairs were too challenging and he was telling me I was a wuss because I didn't push myself one last day above 26,000 feet. As if there was nothing to it.

But the worst part, I sort of agreed with him. I should have gone for it. I was standing there at LAX thinking, "This is what it's going to be like coming home."

MAGGIE'S REBUTTAL

The opinion of the customs officer wouldn't be unique. Most people can't understand what it feels like to climb above 8,000 meters, into the Death Zone. It's not a walk in the park.

On the flight from Los Angeles to Pittsburgh, I got a little reprieve. I was seated next to a sweet woman who was an actress. She told me about the various roles she'd been in, but then she wondered about me. She asked where I was coming from, what I'd been up to. When I told her about Everest, she said, "That's awesome." She was a whole lot nicer than the jerk at LAX customs.

Waiting in Pittsburgh, I was so close. I couldn't wait to get home. When I arrived in Rochester, though, everything was a fog. It was nice to have people there to greet me—

my brother Chris, my friends Forest McMullin and Gary Fallesen, and Maggie, of course. I kissed her and hugged her. "Don't worry," I whispered, "I'm done with big mountains forever."

The following day Maggie told me about an Atlanta sportswriter who'd written some derogatory comments about May 16 on Everest, which turned out to be a perfect day with more people making it to the summit on one day than ever before. In all, 61 made it from the South Col and another 19 came up from the Tibetan side. The writer, trying to be funny, said it wasn't such a big deal to climb the Big E these days. He said there was probably a Starbucks at Base Camp and an escalator that went all the way to the top. When Maggie read this, she was ticked. No, she was livid. She e-mailed him about how hard I'd worked and that climbing Everest had been my dream. She was very protective of me.

In her response, she wrote, "I hope he goes back and does it."

When she told me this, I said, "What, are you nuts? You would want me to go away for that long again? No way. I'm not going back. I'm done with big mountains."

THE CURE DOESN'T TAKE

When I got back, our office had moved. Work was going well and we'd needed bigger space. I walked in the first day, like, "Where do I work? Which one is my office?" It was all set up for me. So, I had missed all of that pesky moving, which wasn't a bad thing.

It was good to be back at work, but I was in a daze. I'd read that it takes 21 days to break or make a new habit. Having been on the mountain 60 days, I was accustomed to that lifestyle. It was going to take a while to get reacclimated to my old lifestyle. Plus, I was depressed. People said I was really out of it. I don't think I was myself for at least a month. You put so much of yourself into a climb like that—your time, energy, money and ego—and then it doesn't turn out how you planned. I was struggling with that.

Both of my partners, Ray and Chris, told me that if I wanted to go back they'd support me. I was touched by this. They would have to cover my butt and, besides, I'd get paid while I was off climbing. But I told them they didn't have to worry. "I'm not going back," I said, yet again. "I'm done."

Then I started to replay the tapes in my head. If I could have done this or if I could have done that. I kept thinking about the move from Camp 3 to Camp 4 and what Rob Link had told me. I started thinking, "I was pretty close. If I'd felt better, I could have done it." It started to eat at me. I was close and I could have done it.

Then it hit me. Before, I wanted to climb Mount Everest. But now, with the support and encouragement of my wife and business partners, I needed to do Everest. There are two choices you don't own: when you're born and when you die. Everything else is about choices. You can do all sorts of things if you put your mind to getting them done. About two weeks after I got back I started thinking I could make a better attempt at climbing Everest. I thought about Eric's e-mail from before, when he suggested going to Cho Oyu because it was lower and you don't spend as much time and money. Ted and Stuart had both done that. They were prepared. I started thinking that maybe the experience of having attempted Everest could work out. McKinley and Aconcagua had been that way. I'd failed the first time and summitted the second time on both of those peaks.

The depression and anger turned into resolution. I came to grips with Simonson's decision making. He wasn't the one who stayed in the tent at High Camp. It was up to me to be ready to go. I vowed that I would go back and get out of the tent. I would answer the bell.

On June 23, Gary Fallesen wrote a story in the Rochester newspaper about my climb. Like my wife and my business partners, he knew I was going back before I did. At the end of the story he wrote:

No more big peaks? No more climbs over 20,000 feet?
"I'm giving strong consideration to going back in 2004,"
Flynn said.
He's not done yet.

In July of 2002, I saw Eric Simonson at the Outdoor Retail Show in Salt Lake City. We had lunch. It was good to see him. I told him I couldn't go in 2003 but I was aiming for 2004. We talked all about it. He talked about my having more experience being a good thing. He said I was good teammate. I remember talking to him about leaving Camp 3. That was one of those important moments that didn't work—the goggles fogging up, panicking me, freaking me out. He told me, "The first time using oxygen is tough." I started thinking about logistics. Go to Camp 3, spend one night without oxygen to shock the red blood cells, then get up in the morning and put on oxygen and hike up above Camp 3. Just a practice run. Come back to Camp 3 and spend the night breathing Os.

I knew I could train better. I'd know the drill better. I knew I wouldn't be happy if I didn't go back and at least give it a shot. Otherwise, I'd always be second-guessing myself. I couldn't live with not getting out of the tent on summit day. I thought the next time I could get it right.

That's when I decided I was going to go back. So much for the cure.

ANGER TURNS TO RESOLUTION

You look for excuses or for a scapegoat. It takes a long time for your fragile ego to acknowledge that the problem was you. It wasn't Eric. It wasn't the weather. It wasn't my goggles. All of that might have contributed to it, but ultimately it came down to this: it wasn't Simo's fault and it wasn't Tucker's fault for telling me to conserve my oxygen. It wasn't anyone else's fault.

I finally took responsibility. I was angry about a lot of things, but in the end it was up to me to climb to the top of that mountain. I realized that. I came to my senses and I admitted defeat.

When I decided to go back to try to climb Everest again, all of that bad stuff was accepted. I came to grips with my failure. Then I decided to try to do everything better. I would be smarter. I would be mentally tougher. I would be stronger.

I felt badly for blaming other folks. I, and I alone, was to blame for not making the summit.

Maggie and I talked. She knew I needed to go back. It was like a burr under my saddle. If I never, ever got up Everest, would this be a bad life? Of course not. But there was a little hollowness in my soul. A void. She knew it was a big deal.

I wasn't sure if I would be ready to go back the next year. I wanted to give a breather to my partners. If I had climbed the next year, I would have been gone for five of 15 months to make the two attempts. That's a long time to be away from work. I wanted to train, too. Hard. And I wanted to enjoy spring. It just felt right to give it a little bit of time.

The first time I went to Mount McKinley, three and one half weeks away seemed irresponsible and wrong. It seemed like such a long time. Then to not summit and want to go back; it was funny how people worked to accommodate me. It was great that Maggie, Chris and Ray were so supportive of my plans for Everest in 2004.

My only concern was my age. When I left in 2002, I was 44. This time, I'd be 46 and turn 47 on the mountain. I wasn't getting any younger. Although I knew of some much older climbers who had summitted.

In the back of my mind, I knew I wanted to get to the summit. But, more so, I just wanted to answer the bell. Getting out of the tent was the biggest demon I wanted to exorcize. I felt like a fighter who'd fought a good fight and then didn't come out for the final round. No mas. Friends asked if it bugged me, not getting to the summit. I joked, "I hardly even think about it anymore. Only about 15 or 20 times a day." Only I wasn't joking. It was sort of haunting.

PREPARING FOR EVEREST—
AN ADIRONDACK ADVENTURE

I didn't go back to the gym until Dec. 4, 2002. Mostly I took off the summer and fall of 2002. I tried to get back to work and back to a normal life. I played some golf. Hey, I wasn't a total couch potato; I carried my bag. It probably took my knee about 10 weeks to heal. I had fluid on it, but it resolved itself in time.

That summer, in August, Maggie and I went to the Adirondacks to climb Redfield and Cliff, two trail-less peaks. They were Maggie's forty-first and forty-second 4,000-footers on her way to the Adirondack Forty-Sixer Club. Redfield had been my first trail-less peak many, many years before. I wasn't good at route-finding way back then. I probably spent eight or ten hours on a terrible day trying to find and stay on the herd path to the top. The day Maggie and I did it, it was a spectacular day. We made great time on our way up.

Now I have a propensity for turning my ankles. We were about as far away and as deeply in as you can get when I twisted an ankle and went down like a sack of potatoes. There I was writhing in agony. There was the immediate white heat of pain with Maggie looking down at me. I didn't know how badly it was hurt. When I put weight on it, I could feel that it was sprained. But it wasn't the worse sprain I'd ever had. Maggie, who is a certified athletic trainer, had some tape with her and she did a great job taping me up. I felt badly, though, that we wouldn't be able to do Cliff.

Then when we got to the junction where you either head up Cliff or start hiking out, I thought, "My ankle's not that bad." There was this person coming off Cliff and he was talking about all the blowdown from an ice storm the winter before. "Oh, my gosh, it's terrible," he said about the route up Cliff. "You'll be lucky to find your way." We made it fine. Of course, I was hopping along. Here's the big Everest veteran, gimping through the Adirondacks.

We were sleeping in a lean-to and I knew the next day we would be carrying full packs for five and one half miles. I was thinking, "This is not going to be fun." We had reservations at a fancy lodge and we were planning on playing some golf. We were going to enjoy the cushy life for a few days after our backcountry adventure.

That night, at camp, we cut the tape off and I soaked my ankle in the river. It was puffed up the next morning, but it wasn't ridiculous. With my trekking poles, I knew I could support it. I thought, "OK, this is doable and, most importantly, I haven't ruined the weekend." Besides, I figured it would help toughen me up for Everest.

Maggie was leading and we'd crossed the tricky terrain. We had about two miles of easy walking ahead of us. Maggie went over a log for fun and, then, she slipped. Fortunately, she was able to break the fall—with her nose on a large boulder. I watched the whole thing in horror. She let out this really frightened scream. I limp-ran up to her not knowing how bad it was going to be. She'd just hit her head on a rock.

There was blood everywhere. It appeared to be pretty bad. She asked me, "How does it look?" I knew she was going to see herself in a mirror in the car in a little while, so I figured I better be honest. "Honey," I told her, "it looks really bad. But there's plastic surgery. They can fix you up." She looked like she'd gotten hit by Mike Tyson or something.

She's pretty tough and she cowboyed up after a while. I was thinking, "This is great, now we're both hurt." I didn't know if I'd have to carry her out, and I didn't know if I'd be able to with my sprained ankle. She said she could make it and we continued on looking like the Fife and Drum Bugle Corps—me limping and her all bloody.

When we finally got to the car, she looked at herself and announced, "Wow, this doesn't look so bad." It wasn't that pretty, but she'd expected the worst. We went to a hospital near Lake Placid, where they took X-rays of her nose. They made it official, declaring it broken. But there was nothing they could do about it with all the swelling. So we drove back to the fancy lodge where we were going to stay. I limped up to the front desk followed by this woman who was still all bloody. We looked as if we'd been in a car wreck. We got in our room and had our bottle of champagne. We cleaned up. We even played golf the next couple of days. Of course, I took a cart.

That was part of my preparation for Everest.

I was thinking, "Every time I climb a mountain, there's something. Whether it's Everest or in the Adirondacks." I was tired of limping away from mountains.

THE ADVANTAGES OF FAILURE

There are advantages to failing. Because of my experience on Everest in 2002, I knew how to work out better—cardio five times a week and weights three times. Failure does suck, but it doesn't kill you. It's like that in business, too. You learn and improve. If you can fail and it doesn't put you out of business, it's going to make you better. Same thing with flying. If you find yourself in situations when the old pucker factor comes up and you learn from those experiences, you're usually a better pilot for it. There are times to push it. Being an entrepreneur, a pilot, a mountaineer, there are risks involved. You learn when to push and when to back off.

I knew in my mind that the move from Camp 3 to Camp 4 had to be done earlier in the day. The mystery of the Icefall had been removed. I'd been through a storm. I'd made some bad decisions up high. There was no more mystery between Base Camp and Camp 4. All the mystery, for me, was above Camp 4. But I figured I would be ready to face that. The second time seemed to be the charm. It had worked on McKinley and on Aconcagua. Learning from experiences turned failure into an advantage.

I got some nice e-mails from Stuart Smith when I was wondering if I should go. Short and to the point. He wouldn't start off with a "Hi, Kevin" or any other pleasantries.

"Hey, look, I've heard your chances of summitting double the second time you're there," he would write. "Are you going back?"

I'd reply, "Well, yeah, I'm thinking of going."

"Go," he wrote back. "You know you need to."

Stuart's a lawyer from Waco, Texas, with a real economy of language. But I liked what he was saying.

I thought to myself, "Damn it, at least I'll get out of the tent the next time." What hurt the most was that I never gave it a shot. Even if I'd gone up and turned around at The Balcony—but I didn't even leave High Camp. I'd tell people that and they'd say, "Bad weather?" No. "Sick?" Well, not exactly. Just exhausted. "Exhausted?" I Monday-morning-quarterbacked this thing eight ways to Sunday. Was that an excuse? Did I not have the resolve?

TO RUSSIA WITH LOVE

As our old 707 plane touched down at the St. Petersburg airport, I peered out the tiny jet window and wondered what kind of reception awaited us in Russia. I remembered spending about half of my time in the second grade under my desk practicing "duck-and-cover" drills, preparing for the imminent, incoming Soviet nuclear bombs.

It was July 2003. I still had the Seven Summits dream in my head. Since I was going back to Everest in 2004, I'd decided to climb Russia's 18,481-foot Mount Elbrus, the highest peak in Europe. I figured it would be a good intermediate mountain. It would be a nice way to gauge how the training was going. And, of course, it was one of the Seven Summits.

Everything I'd heard about Elbrus was that it wasn't that pretty. But it's in the beautiful Caucuses. I didn't know how pretty it would be.

I also had no idea how the Russian people would act toward us. In my mind, I'd guessed they wouldn't like us. Instead, our Russian guide Igor greeted us with smiles. He could not have been nicer.

I went to Elbrus with IMG and Phil Ershler. I knew I could do this mountain on my own. It's pretty straightforward, though summit day is a big day (a 5,000-foot ascent and a round-trip that takes about 13 hours) and it can have some nasty weather. But the fact that Ersh was leading and that I could be around him and learn from him was the reason why I decided to go with IMG. I was also reunited with Stuart Smith on this trip.

We spent a couple of days in St. Petersburg, sightseeing and soaking up some of the culture. Normally, I'm psyched to get to the mountain ASAP and start the acclimatization process, but St. Petersburg was a brilliant distraction. Not that I was the average tourist. I was up at five in the morning running five miles through this city of bridges, which is known as the Venice of the North. I knew I was supposed to be able to skip up this mountain, being an Everest vet, but it was still an 18,000-foot peak. I'd been back in the gym, training pretty hard. I was working out harder than I had for my first Everest attempt.

When Ersh started giving our group of twelve climbers instructions, he'd turn to Stuart and me and say, "Of course, you guys know this." On the mountain, he'd ask everyone, "How are you feeling? Not you guys. You better feel OK."

I started feeling a little pressure. I was thinking, "What

if I flame out on Elbrus, which is barely above Everest Base Camp?"

On our sixth day in Russia, we loaded into buses and were transported to the foot of Elbrus, which is at 7,500 feet. The lower part of the mountain is a ski area. From the base, we took two gondola rides up the mountain, followed by a single chairlift to 12,500 feet. Not a bad way to start a climb.

We hiked up a snowfield for a couple of hours to reach huts at 13,700 feet. This would be our base camp for three nights. On summit day, we awoke at 12:30 a.m. and set out by 2. It was earlier than most parties start, but Ersh wanted to give the group some extra time to enhance the chances of everyone making it to the top.

At the beginning we were moving impossibly slow. Ersh wanted to keep the whole team together. But we were going so slowly that I was getting cold. I was beginning to think, "Dude, spin some of these people or, better yet, let us go on ahead." Stuart and I were talking about it while we waited. I told Stuart to ask Ersh if we could split up. He said, "I'm not going to ask him, you ask him." When Ersh came along, Stuart said, "Kevin wants to know if we can split the group up." Ersh gave me a dirty look while Stuart suppressed a smile. Thanks a lot Stuart.

Phil kept us together until about 7 in the morning when he decided to let us go ahead. We climbed up to a saddle about 1,000 feet below the summit, where we were supposed to wait for the rest of the group. Surprisingly, everyone made it up about 45 minutes after us, including the slowest climbers. Ersh came in with them offering advice and encouragement. Unbelievable. He was going to get the weakest climbers to the summit. Vintage Phil.

The upper 1,000 feet are the steepest part of the climb. I'd been videotaping the climb and I wanted to be on the summit first so I could record everyone arriving. I made my way up as quickly as possible. The lack of oxygen and fairly steep terrain kept my pace slow, but steady. At 10:30 a.m., I stepped on the rooftop of Europe. It's always an exhilarating feeling to reach the top and I had the chance to document everyone enjoying his or her moment of glory. The entire group summitted.

We descended back to the hut by mid-afternoon without incident. Ersh was about an hour behind with the two slowest climbers. He was carrying his pack along with the two other packs on his back. Typical. The following day, we hiked down to the chairlift and gondolas and enjoyed the ride off the mountain.

When we got back in the Baskan Valley, I ran up about 3,000 feet to shoot some video. I humped up there in a couple of hours. I was in a rhythm, in a groove. The machine was working. I did it before breakfast, then we went ice climbing. It felt good. As a mid-way checkpoint in getting ready for Everest, I thought, "Yes, the training is going the way I want it to go." I already felt I was in better shape than when I went to Everest the first time.

More importantly, it was fun to be successful again on a mountain. I didn't limp off Elbrus. It reaffirmed all the things I loved about climbing—being with great people, on a nice mountain, and pushing myself a little. It was the perfect way to get excited about going back to Everest. Nothing could stop me now.

MY DAD'S DYING

"The man of the hour is taking his final bow. As the curtain comes down, I feel that this is just goodbye for now."

– Pearl Jam, *"Man of the Hour"*

My dad, Jerry, was the man of the hour. He was the coolest guy I ever knew, a hometown celebrity. He was a toastmaster for hundreds of sports banquets so, as a kid growing up, I always saw him with all these big-name athletes—from Terry Bradshaw to Mickey Mantle to Jack Nicklaus to Muhammad Ali. It was really impressive that all these sports superstars knew my dad. In fact, his first sports dinner appearance was with an aging Cy Young.

Jerry Flynn grew up in a poor, working class Irish family.

He was born in the United States, but his family moved back to Ireland when he was two or three. His father was involved with the IRA and was almost shot by the British Army. His wife intervened and the family had to move back to the United States when Jerry was five. He was the first member of his family to go to college. He went to Notre Dame. He was very popular, became the head cheerleader and traveled with the football team. In those days, they traveled by train. They made these whistle-stops in small towns across the Midwest and he would pretend he was a famous fullback, even though he was only 5-foot-7, 130 pounds. He'd sign autographs, shake hands and pose for pictures. With no TV then, no one knew. "I made people happy in all these little towns," he used to say. He was quite the character. He and another cheerleader friend of his would take the Notre Dame mascot, a little Irish Terrier dog, out to local bars the night before games. The bar patrons would inquire about the dog. That always led to an explanation about their affiliation with the Fighting Irish football team. Then the locals—enamored with the Notre Dame mystique—would buy them free drinks all night. During games, the dog would be asleep on the sideline under the bench because they had kept him out all night.

After college, he joined the Navy during World War II. He served on the U.S.S. Enterprise and won 11 battle stars. He was the morale officer, of course. They couldn't drink on the ship, so he would coordinate R&R with about a million bottles of beer for his men on the local islands in the Pacific.

After World War II, he became Sports Information Director at the Naval Academy. That was back in the day when the Army-Navy football game was the Super Bowl. He spent time in New York with all the famous sportswriters.

Eventually he came back to Rochester and worked in advertising sales and later started his own ad agency. He taught me business ethics on a high level. He also did about 3,000 speaking engagements. He and my mom were soul mates for 47 years. Mom died March 14, 2000. She'd been diagnosed with lung cancer in the early part of December 1999. Gary Fallesen and I were planning to climb Aconcagua in January 2000. We delayed the climb a year. I remember knowing it was the right decision not to go.

My dad had had multiple bouts with cancer. He had cancer of the vocal chords in 1975 and lost his voice box in 1991. He would speak to middle school classes and show them the hole in this throat and talk about the dangers of smoking. I think he enjoyed it as much as sitting next to a Wayne Gretzky at a sports dinner.

But at the end of 2003, my father's health took a turn for the worse. The machine was just starting to wear out. He and I were the same height 10 years before he died. We were both 5-foot-9. But by 2003, he was about 5-foot-5 and all hunched over. The bones were starting to go bad. During his last six months, his quality of life was poor. But he never complained. In fact, it was difficult to remember that he was sick.

I'd never been worried about him in the past. "We'll just beat this," he'd always say. If he wasn't too worried about it, I wasn't worried. The difference this time, he was getting ready to go.

In January 2004, he was recovering from surgery on his bladder at a rehabilitation medical facility. They found fluid in his lungs. It was non-symptomatic pneumonia. At this point, he was 84-years-old and weighed 125 pounds. On

Thursday, January 22, he called us all in—my sister Colleen, my brothers Kerry and Chris, and our spouses. He walked into this little meeting room. The medical-case worker explained the situation.

"I've made a choice," he told us. "I'm not going to take any medications. The reason I asked you all in here is to tell you that I love you all very much. I've had a wonderful life. No regrets. Don't cry over me. I'm ready."

Of course, everyone cried.

He wanted to go stay in the Genesee Hospice, where my mom died. The nurses there were absolute angels in the treatment of my mom. At that point we didn't know how long he had. Selfishly—and I'm embarrassed to admit this—I was torn between whether or not to continue with my plan to climb Everest. I'd been training so hard and I didn't want anything to keep me from the climb. But I couldn't imagine what it would be like to be on the mountain if my dad died.

The next day, Friday, we went to visit. He was hardly talking, which was unusual. He would just wave. On Saturday, nurse Denise McNulty, who'd taken care of my mom, was going to evaluate him. That night or Sunday morning he was no longer communicative. He was basically not awake. Monday morning his vitals were not great, but good enough to transfer him to the hospice. An ambulance came to take him there. The driver let me sit in the back with him and hold his hand. It was against the rules, but he made an exception.

Unfortunately, my brother Kerry had to go away on a business trip just a day earlier. No one knew it was going to be this fast. But suddenly we were on a death vigil. Kerry called from the airport in Washington D.C. He wanted to be with us so bad, but he was delayed by weather. It was heartbreaking and frustrating for him. The nurse told my dad, "Your son is trying to make it back, Jerry. But because of the weather he can't be here." The nurse held the phone to my dad's ear so Kerry could say goodbye. "I love you, I'm trying to get home, but it's OK for you to go."

It was an amazingly short period of time. About a half an hour later he started to take his last breaths. Chris' oldest daughter Katie had written a poem and read it for him. There was a calmness and serenity and resolve about him. He'd made his decision. No one thought it was going to be days instead of weeks. But he was so strong-willed. He was ready.

I remember a few days before he'd said to me, "What's my timetable here, pal?"

"I don't know, buddy," I'd told him. "You're supposed to live forever."

His dying was a very surreal kind of thing. He went very peacefully and quietly.

In typical Jerry fashion, he had donated his body to science. He felt the medical profession had been so good to him and had given him a number of second chances.

He was one of the lead stories on TV and in the newspaper. He didn't want a funeral, he wanted a celebration. He had given us his instructions.

"What I'd like to do is have a party, with good food and drinks for folks," he had told us. "Make sure it's a helluva party with good music—Frank Sinatra, Glenn Miller, Tony Bennett, and Dean Martin."

About every tenth song in the loop we threw in the Notre Dame fight song. It was a true celebration of life. There were tears, but there was more laughter than tears. It would have only been better if he were there. And I'm sure he was.

Dad died on January 26—seven and a half weeks before I was scheduled to leave for Everest.

HERE WE GO AGAIN

"I find I'm so excited I can barely sit still or hold a thought in my head. I think it's the excitement that only a free man can feel. A free man at the start of a long journey whose conclusion is uncertain."
– Red from *Shawshank Redemption*

I remember going to the gym, listening to a melancholy song, October Project's *Return to Me*. I was doing the StairMaster with tears running down my face. After a serious time of reflection about my dad, it was again time to look forward. I had seven weeks to go.

It's funny how time just accelerates and gets compacted. It's the Venturi effect in your life. It's hard because you have to prepare for all the things that are going to come up. After

March 18, when the plane leaves, there's nothing more that can be done to get ready for Everest or in my personal and business life.

I always liked that quote from the *Shawshank Redemption*, where Red is talking about the start of a long journey whose conclusion is uncertain. That sums up adventure. I knew people had gone up this trail before. Climbing the south side of Everest wasn't new, but it was new to me. I hadn't been up those last 3,000 feet.

This time I was more resolved. The trepidation from the previous trip was replaced by joy and excitement to get going and get back at it. I knew I was going to enjoy the trek more. I wasn't worried about the Maoists. I was there to enjoy it from the get-go. The angst and worry—all that energy spent on the worry—was gone. The first time was nervous and exciting. This time was just exciting.

Mark Holbrook, an old friend, was going to make the trek into Base Camp with me. My only real worry was he hadn't been that high before. He'd done a couple of 14ers 30 years ago. To get ready for the trek, he'd done one backpacking trip in the Adirondacks. I have this propensity to wax poetic, "Dude, you'll love it. You should go." I got him all jazzed on it. He was in his early 50s at the time. He worked out. But his real experience had been a two- or three-night outing in the Adirondacks. I felt a teeny bit nervous for him.

We left on March 19, flying from Rochester to New York City. This time there were no tears at the airport. I don't want to say it was more casual, but it was more casual. "OK, I'm going back to Everest."

Maggie did tell me I still owed her 36 years. When we got married, we joked that this was a 50-year deal and then

SUMMIT
29,035 feet

CAMP 4
26,200 feet

CAMP 3
24,080 feet

CAMP 2
21,300 feet

CAMP 1
20,000 feet

BASE CAMP
17,500 feet

KALA PATTAR • --- • MT. EVEREST
GORAK SHEP • EVEREST
                 BASE CAMP
LOBUCHE •   CHUKHUNG RI

         TUGLHA
PHERICHE • • DINGBOCHE

      • PANGBOCHE
   • TENGBOCHE
• NAMCHE BAZAR

• PHAKDING

LUKLA

TOP Mount Everest camps, south side.

*INSET Trekking map shows the 35-mile trek
from Lukla to Everest Base Camp.*

ABOVE *The 2002 IMG team from left to right: Ted Wheeler, Mark Tucker, Eric Simonson, Stuart Smith, Dr. Lee Meyer, me, Susan Ershler, and Phil Ershler.* (Photo: Stuart Smith)

LEFT *Simo took this picture of us at Base Camp at 5 a.m. on May 11, 2002, just as we were about to start our summit run. From left to right: Phil and Susan Ershler, Mark Tucker, Stuart Smith, Ted Wheeler and me.* (Photo: Stuart Smith)

TOP *Welcome to Lukla Airport. The approach to landing is always exciting.*

ABOVE *Porters help carry our supplies along the trekking route.*

RIGHT *Most porters have reasonable footwear — but not this fellow.*

ABOVE *I'm at the entrance to Sagarmatha National Park.*

ABOVE *Porters and yaks cross a bridge on the way to Namche Bazar.*

LEFT *Nepali Army patrol near Phakding keeps the Maoists at bay. Their presence was reassuring but also made me anxious.*

BELOW *The beautiful village of Namche Bazar, the Sherpa capital of the Khumbu Valley.*

LEFT *Our first look at Everest from just beyond Namche. The jet stream creates a three mile plume of snow off the summit.* (Photo: Jason Tanguay)

BELOW *A telephoto view of the upper reaches of Everest. Very pretty and kind of scary.* (Photo: Jason Tanguay)

Jason Tanguay flies his kite during a lunch break near the village of Pangboche. Mount Ama Dablam is in the background.

LEFT *Sherpa children take turns flying Tanguay's kite.*

BELOW *Mark Holbrook and I enjoy the 18,400 foot summit of Kala Patar.*

LEFT *The wreckage from a Russian M16 helicopter that crashed near Base Camp in 2003. Three people were killed in the crash.*

ABOVE *The 2004 IMG High altitude Sherpa team and non-guided climbers— all 28 of us. Only five climbers and two Sherpas would make the summit.*

RIGHT *I'm flanked by Susan and Phil Ershler, the first married couple to do the seven summits. I'm wearing Phil's "reindeer copulation" hat, something he lent me for its good summit karma.*

ABOVE *Right after we arrived at Base Camp in 2004 we helped smooth out a helicopter landing area. The Khumbu Icefall is visible in the background.*

RIGHT *Ladders lashed together make the going easier through the Icefall.*
(Photo: Brien Sheedy)

BELOW *Near the top of the icefall.*
(Photo: Jason Tanguay)

ABOVE *Ladder crossing over a crevasse. We got used to these crossings but they were never quite casual.*
(Photo: Brien Sheedy)

RIGHT *I'm negotiating jumbled ice blocks. This section had fallen apart just days before this crossing.*
(Photo: Brien Sheedy)

BELOW *Brien Sheedy inside the mess tent at Camp 2.*

LEFT *I'm arm-rappeling down the Lhotse Face just below Camp 3 at about 24,000 feet.* (Photo: Jason Tanguay)

BELOW *Inside my tent at Camp 3 signaling "2" and "4" to celebrate reaching 24,000 feet.*

LEFT *Frosty the Snowman, with his perpetual grin, was where Mark Tucker and I kept track of our card playing gambling debts.*

BELOW *That's me playing a little golf at the "Khumbu Country Club."*
(Photo: Mark Tucker)

OPPOSITE LEFT *A couple of our tents at Camp 3 dug into the Lhotse Face. Notice the safety lines around the tent. A slip here would be fatal.* (Photo: Jason Tanguay)

OPPOSITE RIGHT *Climbers ascending above Camp 3 towards the Yellow Band.*

ABOVE *Mark Tucker draws a poor lie.*
"Let's see, if the ball is above the feet,
you tend to pull it..."

LEFT *Ron Hauglin makes his way up*
the Yellow Band. (Photo: Brien Sheedy)

BELOW *Brien Sheedy takes a rest at the*
base of the Geneva Spur.

BOVE *Dan Barter takes five at the*
Geneva Spur. It's hard to see individual
ces so we'd just identify our fellow
limbers by their clothes and backpack.

IGHT *Me near the top of the Yellow*
Band at around 25,000 feet.
(Photo: Brien Sheedy)

ELOW *Dan Barter and I ascend the*
Geneva Spur just below 26,000 feet.
(Photo: Brien Sheedy)

LEFT *Tents at Camp 4, the South Col at 26,200 feet.*

BELOW *Dan Barter looking chipper after arriving at High Camp on Friday May 14, 2004.*

BOTTOM *That's me on summit day just above the Balcony at around 27,700 feet. Mingma Tshering is just barely visible behind me wearing yellow.*
(Photo: Jason Tanguay)

ABOVE *Climbers making their way up towards the South Summit on May 15. We were among the first groups to attempt Everest in 2004.*

BELOW *Karma Rita adjusts his gloves somewhere above the Balcony. Makalu, the world's fifth tallest mountain is in view and you can almost see the curvature of the earth from here.*

ABOVE *View of the traverse, the Hillary Step and the true summit as seen from the 28,750 foot South Summit.*
(Photo: Jason Tanguay)

RIGHT *My hero, Mingma Tshering Sherpa on the summit of Mount Everest.*

Here I am
looking rather grim on
the summit of Everest.
(Photo: Mingma Tshering Sherpa)

RIGHT I'm flanked by compadres Dan
Barter (left) and Brien Sheedy (right) as
they're waiting for the chopper to fly in
and take me to a clinic in Kathmandu.
(Photo: Mark Tucker)

BELOW Tucker took this shot of Brien
Sheedy and me (left to right) as we
returned to Base Camp from the summit.
It took us two days to get down from
High Camp and I was about ready to
collapse. (Photo: Mark Tucker)

ABOVE Mark Tucker gives me some words
of encouragement as I'm about to board
the chopper and leave Base Camp.
(Photo: Brien Sheedy)

LEFT *Jason Tanguay signs the summit wall of fame at The Rum Doodle Bar and Restaurant in Kathmandu.*
(Photo: Jason Tanguay)

MIDDLE *From left to right: Mark Tucker, Brien Sheedy, Jason Tanguay and Dan Barter at The Rum Doodle showing off the Yeti footprint with all of our names. That footprint would later be glued to the Rum Doodle's ceiling for permanent display. These were my best friends on the mountain and I'm sorry I missed the party but I was already back in the states. They placed my name — rather appropriately — on the pinky toe.*
(Photo: Jason Tanguay)

BELOW *Back home at the Rochester Airport with my wife Maggie — keeping my promise to return home. Some of my nieces and nephews are holding up a congratulatory banner.*

we'd see if we wanted to renew for another 50. At this point, we'd been married 14 years.

From New York, we flew to Vancouver and then to Hong Kong, Bangkok and finally Kathmandu. The Cathay Pacific computer system went down worldwide so they had to check in everyone manually. Our flight left JFK about two and one half hours late. I wasn't worried about getting there; I was worried about my baggage getting there. You can't replace that stuff. But where the last time I was freaking, this time I expected it to work out.

We arrived in Hong Kong at 9:30 a.m. Sunday, March 21. Our flight on Cathay Pacific to Bangkok was scheduled to leave at 9:05 a.m. and it did. However, a Cathay rep met us outside our gate and explained that she'd booked us on the next available flight on Thai Airways. It was not a problem, but they said there was an issue with our baggage. They couldn't locate our stuff. Great. My worst fears were being realized.

Thirty minutes later they came back to us and said, "We've found three of your four bags." I turned to Holbrook and said, only half-kidding, "I hope they're missing yours."

Actually, they had the fourth bag, but it didn't have a tag on it. However, it was clearly marked with my name, so they told me someone from the airline had to escort me out on the tarmac to identify it. They took me down two flights of stairs to the ramp beneath the massive underbelly of our 747. What a thrill that was. Dang, I don't know how those big airplanes get off the ground—and I'm a pilot.

Not long after that we were back on our way. I watched my last bag get loaded onto the plane. What a relief. Everything was going to be OK.

OLD HOME WEEK

The flight to Kathmandu was uneventful, not that there's anything wrong with that. We arrived and went through the usual craziness getting baggage and getting out of the airport. As I reemerged into the streets of Kathmandu, I had a different perspective. Where before I saw pollution and garbage, this time I saw bustling people and busy shops. Instead of seeing negatives, I was overwhelmed by the positive. I was amazed that these streets—full of bikes, cars, buses and cows—can be an organized chaos. While it looked different to me, everything was familiar and much easier to take.

We were staying again at the Hotel Tibet, where I ran into Mark Tucker. Tuck, who was Simonson's assistant in 2002, was going to be leading the expedition this time around. Simo would be there at the start, but then he would hand us off to Tucker. Tuck and I are kindred spirits, born within a month of each other and with a similar sense of humor. I really liked him and I knew he was going to be fun. As I said before, he's like a big, old camp counselor.

I was introduced to Jason Tanguay, who had won the American Alpine Club's prestigious Sowles Award in 2001 for his role in what became the world's highest mountaineering rescue at 28,750 feet on Everest's North Ridge. I'd read about him and it was nice to meet him in person. He would be assisting Tucker on this expedition.

We got lunch and I had a beer with my meal. This was also different from 2002. But I knew I was in good shape. I'd done my training. Most of the worry was gone. Just excitement. I couldn't wait to get at it. After lunch, I went for a walk around town with Mark Holbrook and Dan Barter, a climber from New Hampshire. Two years before, I had some trepidation about walking around Kathmandu. I still had some small concerns about the Maoist problem, but didn't dwell on it. Now I enjoyed going out and talking to people.

The next day, Tuesday, March 23, Simo came in with Phil and Susan Ershler. It was great to see them all again. Simo was only going to be there long enough to make sure everything was organized, then trek with us to Namche. He would then come back to Kathmandu and get a group ready to go the North Side; then he'd fly home to the states. This was a first for Simo. Normally he led the entire expedition. It would be interesting to see how it would work out.

The Ershlers were leading a trekking group. I was glad I would be with them for part of the trip. I knew there was still more I could learn from Phil and Susan was just very supportive. She was an absolute bundle of excitement.

Because she and Phil turned around at The Balcony in 2001 (when Phil's eyes started to freeze), she could empathize with me about going after it a second time.

"You look like you've been working out," Susan said when she saw me. She went right to work on building my confidence up for the climb. She told me how the second time she tried it everything had seemed so much easier.

That night, we had a climbers-only meeting. It was run by Simo along with Tucker. It was a little bit of an orientation. We had ten non-guided climbers on this trip. Ersh was there to offer support. The three of them—Simo, Ershler and Tucker—all have stood on the summit of Everest. Tanguay had just missed it. I'd been on the mountain before. We all got to share our experiences and what we thought was important about the climb.

After the meeting we went to the Rum Doodle Bar & Restaurant, an institution in Kathmandu. The Rum Doodle was named after the fictitious book by W.E. Bowman, *The Ascent of Rum Doodle*, which was written in 1956 not long after the first ascent of Everest in 1953. The Rum Doodle bar was a piece of mountaineering history because virtually everyone who climbed Everest has been there and signed his or her name on the wall. The original Rum Doodle burned down, but they saved the autographs. The more famous ones—Sir Edmund Hillary and Reinhold Messner—were kept under glass. The deal was that you go there and once you signed the wall and got your Rum Doodle card, you could eat and drink there free forever.

Phil and Susan had to sign in and I got to take photos. Phil, of course, had also signed in years earlier after his first ascent. I felt a great deal of admiration watching them put their names on the wall, alongside all these other people who had climbed Everest. I felt a longing to be a part of that club. That was the first time it hit me. I'd never thought it was that big a deal. But then I could feel an incredible sense of history and I thought to myself, "This is something I want to do—something I need to do." Tucker signed in, too.

In my journal at the end of that day, I wrote:

I will sign my name on that board come the end of May.

I didn't write that I wanted to sign, but that I would sign. It was important for me to write things like that down. Once you write it down, it becomes believable. It's a goal. It's something you can actualize. I was looking forward to being back there in two and one half months to sign in.

But first, I needed a shave.

The next day, after I ran across the road to gamble for forty-five minutes in the casino in the Radisson Hotel (I won $12 U.S.), I bumped into Bill Crouse. He'd been on Everest in 2002 guiding another group. We talked and then I said I was going to go upstairs and shave. I had a five-day growth and we'd be starting our trek to Base Camp soon.

Crouse stopped me. "Have you ever had a real shave, where someone shaves your face with a straight razor?" he asked.

When I said, "No." He told me I had to go get it done.

"It costs like nothing," he said, "and it's a great experience."

I didn't want to go, but he talked me into it. "You're going to thank me," he said, before pointing me in the right direction.

137

The place was only a block from the hotel and while it was hot in Kathmandu, it was cool and air-conditioned in this little shop. I walked in and *Oprah* was on the television. (This city is filled with weird contrasts.) I was worried about sanitation, but the barber showed me how he put a new blade in before shaving my face. Then he went to work. It took forty-five minutes.

He put me in the chair and warmed my face while he took the rubby-dub-dub brush and lathered me up. I have fairly sensitive skin and I thought it was going to hurt, but it didn't. It was probably the best shave I'd ever had. After I thought he was done, he lathered me up and shaved me a second time—even closer than the first time. After that, he soaked my face with a hot towel and put some liniment on my skin and massaged it in. Then he gave me a shoulder rub and massaged my arms. All for 140 rupees, which was less than $2 U.S. I left 500 rupees, which was probably a big tip, about $6 U.S. for me—but nothing compared to what it would have cost back home.

It was really nice to get pampered that way when you knew you were going to be out for the next 50 or 60 days.

This was all part of my enjoying Kathmandu the second time around. Later in the day, Phil and Susan took the trekkers on a six-hour bus tour. I wanted to hang out with my buddy Holbrook and with Phil and Susan so I went along. I was surprised that none of the other climbers wanted to go. We visited the ancient city of Bhaktapur and witnessed a cremation across the river at the Pashupatinath, the most important Hindu temple in Kathmandu, which is closed to foreigners. It was an interesting cultural experience, although I felt a bit like a voyeur looking in on someone's funeral.

Part of going to climb a mountain is trying to drink in some of the culture of the place. The first time I went to Everest, I was so freaked out about it, I didn't see anything. This time was different. I was living in the moment and enjoying it all. Although now it was time to get to work. The next day we would be flying to Lukla to begin our long walk to Base Camp.

TREKKING WITH A PURPOSE

It was exciting to be back, trekking in the Himalaya. We set out on Thursday, March 25 and it was a beautiful day. After my unsuccessful summit attempt in 2002, I was sure I'd never return. But here I was, walking to Phak Ding, as excited as ever. We camped our first night by the river. I beat Tuck in a game of gin before dinner and then shot the breeze with Ershler for a while. He asked me where I was going to have my post-summit celebration party. I think that was his way of giving me encouragement and positive vibes. I was starting to get it, making an attitudinal shift. Two years earlier, I would have said, "Let's not put the cart in front of the horse. If the weather's good and I feel good and if, if, if..." This time I was like, "Yeah, where am I going to have my party?"

I found myself comparing and contrasting everything from 2002 to 2004. How I felt and how I was doing time-wise. Susan Ershler was right about everything seeming easier—so far, anyway. I felt relieved of my mental burden. That needless worry takes energy. I wasn't expending it that way this time around. Plus, I was in better shape. Each day, I would think, "This is a nice little walk. This doesn't seem as long as before."

The difference this time was I wanted to make sure I acclimatized even better. Everest Base Camp is at 17,500 feet, pretty high. But to me, Base Camp was a refuge. Once we got to Base Camp and started the real climbing, I'd be going down to BC. So going up to 17,500 feet didn't seem so high as we were trekking in and up.

On Friday, March 26, we trekked from Phak Ding to Namche Bazaar, climbing up from 8,700 feet to 11,300 feet. On the hike up, I was thinking, "Wow, this is nothing." To gain 2,600 feet and think it was easy was a good sign.

We spent three nights camped at Namche. But I wasn't going to sit around and just enjoy the scene of traders from over the border coming to market. I took a 45 minute walk on the trail to Tengboche and took in the views of Ama Dablam in the morning and in the afternoon hiked up to Syangboche. It took me 45 minutes to gain 1,000 vertical feet. I felt great. I was pushing myself just a little. Before, I might have thought, "Don't use the energy." This time around I knew it was part of the acclimatization. I was making myself stronger.

The next day, Ershler suggested an easy hiking route for the trekkers and said the climbers should go to Thame. It was seven hours round-trip. Only Dan Barter and I wanted to go to Thame, which was sort of surprising. I had been to Thame two years before and it was a pretty good hike. That's the village where Apa Sherpa is from. Apa Sherpa has climbed Everest a record 15 times.

We went to Thame with the studly Sherpa Dorje Llama, who'd been to the summit of Everest with the Ershlers in 2002. Dorje was setting the pace and Barter was an endurance runner, so I knew I would have to work keeping up with these guys. We tore off to Thame with Dorje setting this real strong pace. I was thinking, "This is good." It was 'no worries' to Barter, of course. He would confirm himself as one of the strongest, if not the strongest, Westerner on this expedition. Finally, Dorje said, "You guys are strong." For a Sherpa to say you are fast is a compliment, high praise indeed. I felt like a kid in Little League having the coach tell me I was a good ballplayer. We made it back to Namche in a five-hour round-trip that took me more than seven in 2002.

The next day, Monday, we left Namche for Thangboche, and the following day we reached Dingboche. We were going to spend three nights in Dingboche. In 2002, Ted Wheeler and I hiked about 1,000 feet above Dingboche and I had to go real slow. We turned around before getting to the top of the trekking peak called Bibre. This time, Dan Barter and I decided to go up the same little mountain behind our campsite. The summit of Bibre is at about 16,680 feet. We were just going to hike up and gain some altitude. Well, after one and one half hours we reached the top, having ascended 2,210 feet from camp. That's a pretty good pace. It felt great to get to the top of that little mountain. It's funny about the need to be on top of something. It's tough to explain to someone who doesn't have that I-want-to-get-to-the-top-and-feel-good-getting-there gene. But I was feeling at the top of my game at that point, knowing that the distance between me and Base Camp was growing shorter.

REINDEER COPULATION HAT

When we were climbing Mount Elbrus, Phil Ershler told me I needed to get a hat like his. It was a Wapiti Woolies hat, made in Greenwater, Wash. He called it his "Reindeer (Copulating) hat" (I've cleaned up the language). The design of the hat included a repeated image of two reindeers getting intimate.

"This hat here has good karma," he said. "You've got to get a hat like this."

Well, I thought the reindeer copulating was a bit much. I ordered a nice blue wool hat with snowflakes on it. But this wasn't good enough for Phil.

Somewhere along the trek, he took a good look at my hat and began to question my sexual preference. He kept mocking my hat, saying his was cool and manly and mine was feminine. Finally, one day, he said, "I'll trade you my hat for your hat. This hat's been up there (the summit of Everest). It's got good karma."

My hat was brand new and better looking, but I was happy to trade. I figured it would be sweet to have a summit photo wearing Ershler's hat and then send the dry-cleaned hat back to him. I didn't feel worthy of keeping Phil Ershler's hat. He's one of the superstars in the climbing business.

His willingness to swap hats was just another indication of the consummate guide that he is. One of the things that he's about is helping people get to the top of mountains. He gets great enjoyment from bringing other people success.

The hat swap meant a great deal to me.

The funny thing was, weeks later, after the Ershlers left with the trekkers and we were climbing, I was up at Camp 1 when one of our Sherpas (who was carrying a load of gear up) walked by me wearing my original snowflake hat. Phil gave away my hat after he was done with it. "I knew you'd see your hat on a Sherpa," he said later, "and that would just piss you off."

It made me smile. I had good karma now.

APRIL FOOL'S DAY ON CHUKHUNG RI— OR DAN'S DISAPPOINTMENT

I wanted to get some exercise and Phil Ershler was taking some trekkers up the valley to a small village named Chukhung. It was an hour or two away, about a 500-foot vertical gain. All good. Brien Sheedy and I decided to join them. It was a nice little walk and we got there quickly. So Brien and I thought about climbing Chukhung Ri (Ri means peak). Brien and I didn't look at any maps carefully. Ersh said, "Take Phurba Sherpa with you." We thought the peak was about 17,200 feet and, since Chukhung was about 15,500 feet, we figured it would be a good little hike.

We got up to 17,000 feet and saw that there were two hills ahead of us with a col in between. One hill was higher than the other. We decided to go to the col and see what it was like. When we got there the wind was picking up and it was a lot chillier. I was starting to feel the altitude a little bit.

"Which one should we do?" we asked each other.

Phurba decided for us. "The taller one of course," he said with a grin.

Naturally.

There was a rocky ridge leading up the peak and it got steeper. There were a couple of no-fall zones where slipping would be bad. I was getting a little lightheaded and thinking, "This is much more than we anticipated." Of course, if either dopey me or Brien had looked at the guidebook we would have known.

When we reached the summit, it was a whole lot higher than 17,200 feet. I later learned it was 19,177. We were above Everest Base Camp. We had gained nearly 5,000 feet of elevation. That was much more than we intended. But it was good that we didn't turn around and we were working on getting in a tough mindset.

We left at 9:15 a.m. and returned at 4:15 p.m. It was a butt-kicking day.

Brien and I went into the mess tent when we got back and had a tea and told the story about our day. At dinner, Dan Barter was kind of hurt and peeved at me for not inviting him on our journey. I felt awful. He's a very strong climber and a great guy but I thought we were just going for a little walk. Anyway, I apologized profusely and even though it wasn't my fault, I still felt quite bad.

But I also took it as a compliment that he wanted to be with Brien and me. In a group of 10 climbers, obviously, we weren't all going to climb together. Smaller groups would form from the bigger team.

In 2002, it was mostly Ted, Stuart and I. Phil and Susan

were going to do their thing. Fortunately for me, Ted and Stuart were strong and really great guys. Now I was starting to gravitate toward Brien and Dan.

Three days later, when we were almost to Base Camp, we arrived at Gorak Shep. This would be our last stop before Base Camp. Most of the climbers went up Kala Patar immediately upon reaching Gorak Shep that morning. The Ershlers and most of the trekkers waited until the early afternoon before hiking up Kala Patar. I joined in because I wanted to hike with Mark Holbrook the entire way and share in his shining moment. Kala Patar is an 18,400 foot trekking peak, so it's a pretty big deal. Mark was having one of the best outdoor times of his life on this trek in. I was relieved he was doing so well and enjoying himself, especially since I had encouraged him to do the trek into Everest Base Camp.

Phil asked if I wouldn't mind being the sweep up Kala Patar, making sure the slower trekkers were OK. I was happy to oblige. I was in no hurry and it was kind of fun hanging back and offering encouragement. The views on the way up were stunning, but the clouds rolled in as we got to the summit. I didn't care, it was great fun getting there last and sharing in everyone's success. The group was hugging and slapping hands and taking photos. This was the high point for our trekkers.

When we started heading down, Phil and I walked together behind the group. He was telling me some things about him that I didn't know—about his Crohn's Disease, how sick he was before attempting Everest the first time with Susan in 2001, and how he'd been diagnosed with prostate cancer after Everest in 2002. You look at him; he's the picture of health. He's strong, tough as nails. It made me pause.

He's the Lance Armstrong of mountaineering.

Then the conversation turned to me.

"Who are you thinking of climbing with?" Ershler asked.

"I think the world of Dan Barter and Brien Sheedey's got skills," I said, and Ersh agreed. He called us the "Northeast Contingent" and said we would work well as a team.

"Another guy you want to give consideration to is Jason Tanguay," Ershler said. "He's a guy you want in the trenches with you when the shit hits the fan."

He suggested I stay away from Bruce Bramhill, an Australian, and "Ron" (Rauno) Hauglin, a Finn who lives in Canada. Bruce was a helluva nice guy but he was having trouble just on the trek in and Ron fancied himself a solo climber. I wanted to be around climbers who were team guys. On Everest during the climbing season on the South side, there's really no such thing as a solo climber. Besides, being with people is part of my mountain experience.

I was glad to get Phil's input on the team. We were in agreement. The next day, April 5, we would be completing the trek into Base Camp. Dan, Brien and I hiked in together. We discussed teaming up and everyone liked the idea. The Northeast Contingent was formed. "*Compadre*," Barter started calling each of us.

As we were getting close to Base Camp, we stopped every one hundred yards or so. Just drinking it all in. They were saying, "This is so cool." I was thinking, "Holy, cow, back at Base Camp. Back home."

Then, just before we arrived, we came across a crashed helicopter. Later on, I learned that the accident happened the previous year. Apparently, the chopper brought in some tourists for the 50th anniversary of Norgay and Hillary's first ascent of Everest. I heard that three people had perished and thought, "What a stupid thing it was to bring a helicopter that high."

When we got into Base Camp, Jason Tanguay came by to see me. "Who are you going to climb with?" he asked.

"Dan and Sheedey," I told him.

"Could I climb with you guys?" he asked.

"Are you kidding me? Sure," I said.

The team was set. I couldn't have asked for a better team.

BACK AT BASE CAMP (PUJA TIME AGAIN)

When Dan, Brien and I arrived at Base Camp, we were all giddy. "Can you believe we're here?" After all the months—gosh, years—of training and anticipation, and the 12 days of trekking up, we were finally there. It was a glorious moment, except for seeing the crashed helicopter, which was sobering.

Being back at Base Camp, I knew I would again have my own tent. You need that personal space. On the trek in, I'd shared a two-man tent with Mark Holbrook, which was fun. But now I would have my own place.

On the entire trek in, I'd never felt better. Two years before, I was wondering if I'd even make it to Base Camp. Not this time. Physically, I passed with flying colors. I knew I was acclimatizing much better. Our first dinner at Base Camp was sort of festive, but suddenly I wasn't feeling well. I was afraid I was starting to get sick.

That night, April 5, I didn't sleep well. I had the driest throat I ever remember having. But April 6 was the puja, the Buddhist ceremony in which our expedition was blessed. It started kind of somberly and progressed into a party. In fact, I had three beers, which was probably a mistake being at altitude and considering how my throat was feeling.

The Buddhist monk leading the Puja was assisted by one of our Sherpas named Mingma Tshering. He was the quiet, strong type. I would find out later that he had trained to be a monk for a number of years.

All of the climbers and trekkers were there, except for Ron. "I'm not a Buddhist, I'm not going," he said, which was a major breach of etiquette. You don't have to believe in what they're doing to observe and show respect for the people who are helping you make this climb. After all, we were guests in their country.

As the Puja was happening, a big avalanche let loose. We were in no danger, but it was a big blast. We thought that was auspicious. The Sherpas always take things like that as good signs for the climb ahead. We were happy to accept any sort of indication that our climb would be successful.

This would be our last day with the trekkers. I talked to Phil a lot about acclimatization strategy. I was figuring on two nights at Camp 1 and three at Camp 2 on the first foray up. On the second foray, I wanted to spend a lot of time at Camp 2 (21,300 feet). That's a great place to acclimatize because at Camp 3 (24,000 feet) you are actually starting to deteriorate. I would spend one night at Camp 3 without oxygen, then strap on Os and climb above Camp 3 to get comfortable with the mask. That way it wouldn't be a big mystery and I wouldn't be unfamiliar like I was in 2002. Then, I'd spend another night at Camp 3 breathing Os. Finally, the next time up, I'd go for the summit.

Before making my summit run, I'd rest up at Base Camp. Some people descend even lower on the mountain to heal before making a summit attempt. The disadvantage is you are exposed to a lot of trekkers who may have colds, the flu or intestinal malaise. As soon as we arrived at Base Camp, the joke was that trekkers were disease vectors. Stay away from them. It made me think of Charleton Heston in *Planet of the Apes* saying, "You dirty damn apes." Except, we'd say, "You dirty damn trekkers." We weren't jerks to them. We were cordial. But once you got to Base Camp, if you were healthy, you wanted to stay healthy. There was always a bucket of warm water with soap to wash our hands at the mess tent and we always used hand disinfectant. It was smart to turn into an obsessive/compulsive about personal hygiene.

Ershler was trying to give me as much input as he could before he left. He really liked my strategy, which was actually his from 2002. Before they left, Susan handed out little notes to all the climbers. She and Phil gave me a little silver clover that, unbeknownst to me, they had blessed at the Puja. I was struck by their kind gesture. In my journeys there, Susan had become a big inspiration for me. Phil had given me his hat and provided me with a lot of information, but he was a pro. I was closer to Susan as an amateur climber. I remembered the look of determination I saw on her face during her second attempt in 2002. I think I had the same look this time. She thought so, too. In the note to me, she wrote, "You must know by now, our hearts and hopes are so with you as you reach the top! If you have room in your pack, this (the silver clover) has been blessed. Know when you look at it, Phil and I will be thinking of you."

THE TEAM

Once the trekkers headed out, Base Camp belonged to the climbers. There were 10 of us on this trip, plus Mark Tucker, our expedition leader. Tuck has been a professional guide since 1985. We'd become fast friends in 2002. We played a lot of gin that year and he kicked my butt pretty badly. He was a California boy, a surfer and single. This expedition was a big deal for him to lead because Eric Simonson normally took care of such big groups. Now Simo was back in the States. Simo was arguably the best logistics expert of Himalaya expeditions, so Tuck had some big shoes to fill.

He was being assisted by Jason Tanguay. The "assistant service provider." Tanguay was a 28-year-old science teacher at Vashon High School on Vashon Island off Seattle. He was married. He hadn't been to the summit yet, though he came painfully close in 2001. That was the year they rescued those climbers on the North Side. His behavior during that ordeal far outshined making the summit. Those guys gave up the summit to save lives, while others walked by them on their way to the top. He turned his back on the summit to help others. We knew he was going for the top this time, and we were honored that he'd asked us if he could be a part of the Northeast Contingent.

Tuck and Jason had 10 non-guided climbers to keep an eye on. Besides me, they were:

Dan Barter: A 49-year-old businessman from Manchester, N.H. He was in the silver reclaiming biz. "I'm a glorified junk man," he said. He was also a big-time sailor. He'd climbed McKinley and Aconcagua (though he didn't quite get to the top of the latter because his partner wasn't feeling well). He was super fit. If he wasn't the strongest among us, he was right up there. He'd been a smoke jumper. A super interesting guy. The kind of guy you wanted to have as a climbing partner. He had all the right traits: strong, knowledgeable and a good sense of humor. When he told me how he'd trained, I was suspect. "I wonder if this guy is embellishing," I thought. After I saw him, if anything he'd undersold himself. Plus, he was always positive. You'd ask, "How you doing, Dan?" "Next to the best," he would answer.

Brien Sheedy: A 36-year-old former National Outdoor Leadership Schools (NOLS) leader who'd traveled all over the world. For four or five years, he didn't even have a home—just three or four places where he kept gear, including his parents' house in Syracuse, N.Y. He was a vagabond, a couch surfer. Now he was the Outdoor Recreation Director for Whitman College in Walla Walla, Washington. It's a well-known school in that field. He knew his stuff. He had strong leadership experience in mountaineering, rock climbing, ice climbing and kayaking. He'd studied in Nepal and had been on many trekking peaks. The highest he'd been to was "only" Aconcagua. He was a very strong climber and an all-around great guy.

Bruce Bramhill: Australian. Late 40s. Really nice guy. He'd previously been on the North Side of Everest with IMG attempting the 8,000-meter option. But on the whole trek in, he didn't seem that strong. I didn't think he'd get very high on the mountain. I hoped I would be wrong. I wasn't. He pulled the plug within three or four days after arriving at BC.

"Ron" Rauno Hauglin: Finnish, but lives in Canada. Climbed McKinley five or six times. He was a big-rig truck driver. He'd save up his money and go climb. Ron was very competitive. He was always talking about how fast he did this and that, and how much quicker he did it than everybody else. That said, Ron was quite fit and strong.

Khoo Swee Chiow: Became the first Singaporean national to climb Everest in 1998. He was the first Southeast Asian to complete the Seven Summits. Originally, he was from Malaysia. He was a good guy. He did the peaks and poles (Seven Summits and North and South Poles—also known as the Adventure Grand Slam). Only three others did it before him. He wrote a book, *Journeys to the Ends of the Earth*. His deal on Everest this time was to climb without supplemental oxygen. He was on a bit of a different schedule than us because he was climbing without oxygen. Obviously strong and a good man. I liked him.

Mike Donahoo: Late 40s from the Atlanta area. He

was a lawyer with the United States Court of Appeals for the Eleventh Circuit. That is the Court of Appeals for the Southeast. This was his second attempt on Everest. He turned around somewhere near the Balcony the first time, around 27,500 feet. He was pretty strong and an interesting guy. He could tell an hour-long story at dinner about the Civil War and make it sound really interesting. He was quite intellectual. Yet he could also quote Beavis & Butthead. Now that's a nice balance.

Will Cross and Brad Clement: Will was a Type 1 diabetic. He'd done the North and South Poles and five of the Seven Summits. He was sponsored by the company that made his insulin. Brad was a videographer from Spindrift Films in St. Louis. He was there working for Will. We asked him once, if Will can't make the summit and you can, are you going to go for it? "I'm with him every step of the way. My lot is cast to him."

John Matthews: Early 30s. Colorado. Between jobs. I thought he had an excellent chance, but he spent a lot of time on the satellite phone talking to a girlfriend. He'd been up to Camp 1. His tent got hit with a powder-blast avalanche. I saw him; he looked fine. When we were up at Camp 2 on our first foray he called us to say goodbye. A bit of a mystery to me.

Plus, of course, we had the all-star Sherpa team.

IT SUCKS BEING SICK

I wrote in my journal on Wednesday, April 7:

Felt like crap all day, had a fever (low grade) and my throat hurts. The trekking team left today. Went to the med tent to see what they think. My vitals are OK, but I still feel like shit. I dread leaving the warmth of the mess tent at night for my cold tent. Just need to stay tough.

After feeling killer all the way to Base Camp, I got something. I was trying to be buoyed by the fact that it was early in the expedition. "Better early than late," I told myself. But I was bummed.

Other teammates were going into the Icefall; I felt as if they were getting ahead of me. It sucks being sick on a mountain. You aren't in your own bed. You're trying to eat but you don't have much of an appetite. You have a fever. I would go to dinner at 6 and it would still be light. I'd then return to my cold tent, sick, feeling sorry for myself.

You know you're going to get better, but it's hard to see the end. Dr. Luanne Freer of the Himalayan Rescue Association runs the medical tent on Everest. She's a doctor who works at Yosemite National Park. In 2003, she started setting up an Everest Base Camp medical tent funded by donations. Some expeditions don't have a team doctor; we didn't this time around. I went to see her again on Thursday, April 8. She gave me Zithromax for one day—nothing. I changed to Cipro on my own. At some point, I figured it would kick in.

Some of the battle on the mountain is finding mental toughness when you don't feel well. Brien hadn't been feeling well, either. So we ended up going into the Icefall on the same day—Friday, April 9. I woke up that morning feeling a little better and feeling the need to go for a walk.

In my journal, I wrote:

After awhile I got my act together and went into the Icefall for some practice on the ladders and some much needed exercise. I did fine, but I was slow. I felt so awesome on the trek and now I'm sucking.

The next day, I joined a bunch of people who were building a makeshift helicopter pad in case an emergency heli-evac was needed. Base Camp is like camping out in a rock quarry. But because it's a glacier, it moves. So the rocks are always being redistributed. To make a landing area for a helicopter, they needed to find the flattest possible spot. We spent a good part of the morning moving smaller rocks to fill in the gaps between the bigger rocks. Then you'd get six or eight people to move around these boulders that seemed to weigh a ton.

As a pilot, I was looking at this thing wondering how tricky it would be to land here. I still didn't think it was a very good idea flying up this high. Plus, in the back of my mind was the helicopter that crashed 200 or 300 meters down the glacier.

I had so little energy working on the heli-pad and my throat still hurt. Other climbers were preparing for their first foray higher and I couldn't see my way clear of how bad I was feeling.

In my journal on April 10, I wrote:

Tuck and I play a bunch of games of gin and I actually beat him. Toward the end of my game my stomach starts to rumble and I feel diarrhea coming on. Perfect.

I'm up to four dismal trips to the crapper and my spirits are so low. I miss Maggie. I miss feeling well. I miss home. I miss my dad. I'm definitely questioning why I'm here. I wonder if I'm going to crash and burn. I want to be tough, but it's not easy. I shed a couple of tears of self pity and loneliness. I wish Maggie could hug me and make me feel better.

FIRST FORAY

After a week at Base Camp, I needed a change of scenery. I also needed some exercise. When I was in Base Camp, I had a tendency to lay around. At altitude, the more physical exertion one does, the better. I wanted to get my heart and lungs working. It helps with acclimatizing. I would walk from my tent to the mess tent and feel out of breath. I was beginning to wonder if I was OK. I didn't want to climb up the Icefall—I wanted to limit my exposure to danger as much as possible—so I hiked down toward Gorak Shep. I went alone. It felt good to be moving again.

It's not unusual for climbers to spend their first five to seven days at Base Camp. But, because I'd been sick, I felt as if I was falling behind the others. Several of our team had already begun their first foray. Finally, on April 13, I was ready to make my move.

I wasn't looking forward to our first climb up through the Icefall. Two years before, it had taken forever. The Khumbu Icefall is a scary place to be, especially when you're going too slowly. I was moving through it with Brien, Brad and Will. Our time was really bad.

Brien was leading and I was next. I was slo-o-o-w. Brad and Will weren't going anywhere fast, either. Brien kept stopping and looking back at me with this goofy grin, nodding, as if to say, "Dude, can you believe we're here?" I don't think he was on top of his game. He had also been sick the first few days at Base Camp. But he was doing better than I. Thankfully, he wasn't in any major hurry. When I would take a rest step and lean on my ice ax, breathing hard, Brien was there looking back, grinning and nodding his head. I think he was used to it from his NOLS training; he knew how to hang back with people.

The Icefall is a dynamic beast. You wonder how it's going to change from year to year or even from day to day. It's a 2,000-foot climb with around 25 different ladder crossings. Some are single ladders and some are lashed together to cross larger crevasses. The more that are lashed together the more interesting it gets. The highlight this time around was a four-ladder section that was pretty rickety over one part and shortly thereafter, there were two six-ladder sections, side by side up a big leaning serac. It was a pretty exciting, albeit slow climb up.

Later in the season, I knew some of the ladder spans would change. But I tried not to think too far ahead. You have to stay in the moment and break it down into smaller pieces. It was, at times, terrifying. Quite often, as you were going through the Icefall, you'd hear something crash. "Where is it? Where is it? Phew. OK, it's not going to fall on us." When the frightening sound of a falling serac came from above, I'd hold my breath and hope. Even when the crashing sound was off to the side, I would feel my heart race a little bit. But most of the time the Icefall was utterly beautiful. The scenery was exquisite.

There were many places where I felt exposed and wanted to move quickly. But my pace was mitigated by lack of oxygen. I was always relieved to emerge, unscathed at the top of the Icefall.

On our first foray through there, we carried 35 to 40 pound packs with some stuff that we'd be storing at Camp 1. The first climb up was hard work. We were not used to this altitude yet. Even knowing we were going to have a rest and acclimatization day at Camp 1 didn't help. It took us seven hours to climb through the Icefall.

This did not make Mark Tucker happy. At some point, while we were in Camp 1, he came on the radio and admonished us for our pitiful time.

"Guys, seven or eight hours through the Icefall is pretty bad," he said. "You better do a whole lot better the next time."

I felt pretty lousy when I heard that. Here I was getting over being sick. I'd been trying to dismiss our slow progress in my head, thinking that I wasn't up to speed yet. But Tuck's comment raised the old internal self-doubt again. I was also a little irked. On the trek in, I was smoking. Now, I was among the slowest again.

Fortunately, I felt better going from Camp 1 to Camp 2 (or ABC at 21,300 feet) on April 15. I was starting to feel a little more like myself. I also knew we were going to be in the last tent on the left, just like in 2002, so it made the last 45 minutes of the trip a little less torturous.

While we were there, John Matthews radioed up to say goodbye. Bruce had already left. But John had made nice time up the Icefall and he was doing fine. It befuddled us. You always measure everyone and I thought John had a good chance at making it to the top. He had good experience and was fit and strong. I thought about it, "Bruce has left, John has left. I don't get it." It reinforced some of my self-doubt. "Will I be strong enough?"

Of course, then I thought, "Sweet, there will be more oxygen bottles up high for the rest of us."

You are assigned five or six bottles for the trip. That meant there were an extra 10 or 12 bottles around now. I felt bad that some folks were spinning, but once they've made that decision you can't talk them into staying. It was their decision. They needed to be 100-percent in it. I would miss John, though. I liked him.

April 16 was a lazy day at Camp 2. We played a lot of the card game Hearts in the big dome cook tent. When the sun was out, it could get pretty warm in there. If not, we would put on our baffled down suits. Enjoying the passage of time was important when you had to wait for so much of it to pass. We were amusing the Sherpas with our antics; screaming, swearing and laughing at each other—just yucking it up. The Sherpas looked at us like we were nuts.

We had plenty to eat, too. I think we ate tomato soup, macaroni and cheese and spam for dinner followed by a mixed canned fruit for dessert. Spam tasted good up there.

Brien, Jason, Mike Donahoo and I decided to rope up

on the morning of April 17 to hike up the Western Cwm to the base of the Lhotse Face at 22,000 feet. There was almost no fixed rope from Camp 2 to the start of the Lhotse Face. Sherpas never roped up through there. In 2002, I went through that area a few times unroped, thinking, "This is dumb, this is dumb, this is dumb." On McKinley or Rainier, you would never do that.

The route wasn't really put in yet so we probed our way along, doing well to avoid the crevasses that were all over the place. We moved pretty well as two-man rope teams, then we went back to camp for lunch. Mingmar made homemade chapatis and I stuffed mine with grilled Spam, cheese and mustard—something I'd never do at home. But somehow, up here, it tasted fine. Then we played more Hearts and discussed plans for the next day.

We had intended to return to Base Camp, but some recent collapses in the Icefall had shut down the route. There were three Sherpas, known as "The Icefall Doctors," who were going in to fix the route. But we wondered when. I was anxious to get back to the relatively thick air and cushy lifestyle back down at Base Camp.

We awoke early on Sunday, April 18, and began our descent. The Icefall Doctors were supposed to have the route re-opened by 9 a.m., but we would have to wait and see. We went down to Camp 1. It was cold, clear and windy, but we knew that as soon as the sun would come out we would go from freezing to boiling. It took us about an hour and 10 minutes to get to Camp 1. We crossed three ladders over some big crevasses and rappelled into several other shallower ones to follow our route.

At Camp 1, we radioed Tucker and he said he thought

the Icefall would be opened soon. So we headed down, hoping that he would be right. He was.

Brien and I were moving at the same pace. As we emerged from the Icefall, apparently we looked like real Everest climbers. At least that was what some German trekkers, who were watching us, thought. We were relieved to be through the Icefall; to us it was another successful trip.

As we emerged from the Icefall one of the trekkers asked, "Are you climbers?"

"Um, yeah," I said.

"Can we take your picture?"

Brien and I settled into our roles as high-altitude climbers worthy of being photographed. We had to laugh at ourselves. But we were feeling pretty good after a great first acclimatization foray.

BEATING BASE CAMP BOREDOM

So much of a trip like this was hurry up and wait. We climbed the mountain in slow motion, not only because of the lack of oxygen, but because we had to make a number of forays and needed to recover each time.

A recovery time of five to seven days from a foray up higher was normal. It was hard to eat at that altitude, so when we got back down we ate as much as possible, if only to maintain weight. It was a constant battle to stay as healthy as possible for as long as possible. It was a race against erosion. I felt my quads, which I'd worked on really hard, withering. It was unrealistic to think I could put weight on, but I wanted at least to stop the loss. So a big part of the recovery process was eating. Also, it was a good time to get psyched for going higher.

Base Camp was relatively luxurious. We each had a two-inch thick sleeping pad to put under our sleeping bags. When I would wake up early, I'd listen to my iPod and maybe read a book until the sun hit the tent and started to warm things up. Then, at 8 o'clock, it was time for breakfast. We drank a lot of Sherpa tea and coffee, lots of liquids. We would eat eggs, sometimes French toast with maple syrup, home-fried potatoes, cold cereal, porridge, and Pop Tarts or breakfast bars. I would have a bowl of cereal, the more stupid sugary the better—like Lucky Charms, again something I would never eat at home. I would eat it with powdered milk, which is not on my normal menu, but I got used to it there.

Every 10 days I would take a shower, ladling warm water over myself. I would often take an acclimatization hike or play Hearts with the boys. I played a lot of Gin with Tucker. In 2002, he beat me like a rented mule, and it's not like I'm a bad player. This time I was getting him back. We were playing for a little money. In our mess tent, there was this tacky, little plastic snowman and his hat held lollipops. It was also a good place to keep our scoreboard. I would start to sing *Frosty the Snowman* to remind Tuck that he owed me money. There was a lot of silly, goofy stuff. Grown adults acting like children.

Lunch was served at noon and teatime at three. It was just another opportunity to hydrate and eat. Meals were mandatory unless you were sick. No skipping meals at Everest Base Camp. And there was always food lying around: popcorn, salmon spread in tins and candy bars.

Trying to beat Base Camp boredom was the name of the game. Fortunately for me, the guys I hung out with the most, played cards together in the Mess Tent. I couldn't imagine being stuck at Base Camp with a bunch of jerks. We had a great group. That was part of the camaraderie. I knew at other times we were going to get our tails whipped by the mountain, so it was nice to have a little fun with them, too. It was similar to a foxhole mentality. This wasn't a war, but we were exposing ourselves to danger.

Dinner was at 6 p.m. We usually had nice spirited conversation after dinner until 7:30 or 7:45. Then it was pitch black and I'd go back into my tent alone. It wasn't like I could sleep for 11 hours. So I would take two liters of water, one to drink and one hot. I would put the Nalgene bottle with the hot water between my legs or on my stomach inside the sleeping bag. The warmth from the bottle would help. It was cold in the tent, below freezing. That was home, the place where you spent your evenings. There was no TV, but there was music. My iPod was my salvation. I read a lot, too. Pulpy thrillers. Books like *The Man from St. Petersburg* by Ken Follet. And a bunch of novels by James Patterson. I would strap on my headlamp, read, sit back and chill out. I'd be grooving in my tent. Sometimes I fell asleep with my iPod on.

I had a 5 gig iPod that was recharged with solar power. The iPod people will tell you it only works to 10,000 feet. But it had been working fine at 17,500 foot, our Base Camp.

After the 2002 trip, I planned to take an iPod with much greater storage to Base Camp. I figured, "5 gig good, 40 gig better." I had 900 songs in 2002 and 3,700 songs in 2004, which was only about half full. But on the trek in, my 40 gig iPod crapped the bed. It died. I was complaining to someone about this when I was struck by a bolt of inspiration. I decided to get on the satellite phone and call my brother

Chris at home. He could get me another 40 gig iPod, go to my desktop computer at work and download my songs, then ship it via DHL to Great Escapes Trekking in Kathmandu. (Great Escapes is IMG's in-country connection.) Great Escapes would put the new iPod on a plane to be flown into Lukla, where Phurba Sherpa, our mail runner, would pick up mail and packages to be brought to Base Camp. I figured within a week or 10 days, I could have a new iPod, fully loaded with 3,700 of my favorite tunes. I marveled at my problem-solving ability.

I told Ershler my plan. He looked at me incredulously. Here was this big-mountain veteran who'd lived through the glory days when the climbers actually did most of their own work.

"You know what?" he finally said to me. "You can probably make all that happen. But you shouldn't be able to. It's just not right."

"You're right," I told him. "I shouldn't be able to. But I'm going to."

He just shook his head in dismay. But I had Base Camp boredom to beat.

My new iPod actually reached Base Camp about a week later. The plan worked. For about a day. Then that iPod crapped out, too. Apparently, big hard drives just don't acclimatize as well as humans. So Ershler had the last laugh. (Thank God my 5 gig iPod kept chugging along.)

POTTY TALK

On April 20, I wrote in my journal:

I take a righteous schmoo and notice a bit of bright red blood in my stool.

It was supposed to be a time for R&R. Brien and I were considering making our second foray on April 22 or 23. We were starting to think about the penultimate trip, the last acclimatization hike up high. I hated that this was happening to me, that I had blood in my stool. I hoped that the next day would produce different results.

My journal entry on April 21:

Went to our little stone (outhouse) in the early a.m. I had forgotten about yesterday's episode so I was really bummed when there was more blood in my stool. What's wrong with me? I guess I can't ignore it anymore. I vowed to go to the med tent and talk about my embarrassing problem.

Out bathroom at Base Camp was a little stone hut with a plastic tarp roof erected by the Sherpas. There was a hole in the ground. Underneath the hole was a plastic barrel that held 25 or 30 gallons and could be sealed up pretty well. The barrel was double-bagged with plastic bags. This was our Asian-style bathroom.

Although Base Camp was a rocky area, underneath the moraine was snow and ice—water flowed beneath us during warm afternoons. Dealing with solid human waste is an issue on Everest. Various expeditions pay for a poop porter. Joke to follow: Yes, it's the crappiest job around. When the poop bucket was full, the poop porters would bag it up. They wore masks. It was a nasty job. They were paid $1 a kilogram to carry the human waste down and off the glacier to around Gorak Shep, where they dug a hole and buried it. It was like a landfill. To Nepal's credit, they have been trying to keep Everest as clean as possible and the overall sanitation has improved in recent years at Base Camp.

After the tragedy of 1996, photos appeared of the landscape up high. It was dubbed the world's highest garbage dump. At Camp 4, the South Col, there were hundreds—if not thousands—of empty oxygen canisters littering the area. Cleaning expeditions were sent up. Sherpas were paid a bounty to bring down empty canisters. They would make $15 or $20 per cannister, which was big money for them. Nowadays, expeditions pay a $5,000 deposit on oxygen bottles. If our group went in with 80 bottles and came out with 74, we would have had to pay a penalty from our deposit.

People always wonder about the trash, but the question mountaineers might be asked more than any other is, "Where do you go to the bathroom?"

We had stone outhouses at Base Camp, but up higher we would try to find a crevasse over which we would straddle and go. At Camps 1 and 2 it's easy to find cracks. But Camp 3 is located on a desperate, exposed area. It's a perch. There, you have to hold a garbage bag behind you, go, and then dump it into a crevasse.

That's for No. 2. As for No. 1, there's always the pee bottle. This might be a foreign concept to some, but it's routine for mountaineers.

We needed to drink five or six liters of water per day. It helps the acclimatization process and reduces the chance of hypothermia and frostbite. When I'm a civilian, I sleep through the night. On a mountain, hydrating like that, I would have to go to the bathroom two or three times a night. Instead of leaving the warmth of your sleeping bag, you use a pee bottle. Instead of going outside and freezing, you reach for that specially marked wide-mouthed Nalgene bottle and pee in it. You want to make sure it is clearly marked with a "P" because you don't want to mix it up.

Going to the bathroom was a fact of life, and not something that could be taken for granted. Especially when a problem existed.

On the afternoon of April 21, I went to the medical tent to ask about my bleeding backside. You know, you would like to have physical ailments that were a little cooler than this, but what are you going to do? To my surprise, the attending doctor dismissed it. She said that unless I had a family history of polyps or colon cancer or another rectal problem, it was probably just an anal fissure near the end of the line. She explained that up here everyone sat funny on rocks and bathroom habits were off, so it was not uncommon. If I was back home, she said I would probably need a colonoscopy. But things were different here. It likely would resolve itself soon. This encouraged me, especially since Brien and I were now planning to go back up on April 23.

On April 22, I wrote in my journal:

A 'bloodless coup' this a.m. What a nice relief. Plus, a p.m. schmoo with no blood. Nothing is sacred up here, but I'm glad to be rid of the problem—I hope.

SECOND FORAY

I had celebrated my second birthday in three years on the mountain. On April 22, I turned 47. The following day, Brien and I were to begin our second foray. I'd asked him for an extra day in Base Camp to get over my little bleeding problem. Even though I had a bit of the Khumbu cough, I was feeling much better.

There are three keys to climbing Everest: staying healthy, staying focused, and staying mentally tough. Staying healthy is an obvious one. Staying focused is important because it's such a long trip and you don't want to get sloppy. Being mentally tough is something that people don't understand; and it's much more difficult than people would imagine. It's the challenge of being away for so long and thinking about what you would be doing if you were home. I would force myself to remember why I was there: I wanted to climb the mountain.

And so, up we went.

We awoke at 4 a.m. on April 23, hoping to beat the heat of going through the Icefall. I hate to get up early, but it's worth it to get through the Icefall when it's more frozen and the sun doesn't make you feel as if you're an ant under a magnifying glass.

We walked away from Base Camp by 5 a.m. The weather for our move up was not ideal. It was snowing lightly and the visibility was poor. Since dawn was just starting to break, we were wearing headlamps. The weather was atypical for Base Camp. Usually mornings would be clear and then some snow would come in the afternoon. As we ascended, four of our Sherpas turned around. When they retreated to Base Camp, I was concerned. I thought we should turn around. But the Sherpas were more worried about the weather between Camp 1 and Camp 2, not between us and Camp 1, where we were going. Brien reasoned that it wouldn't be as dangerous up to Camp 1. Plus, with the cloud cover, it wouldn't get as hot. So, actually, weather conditions were good for Brien and me.

We made it through the Icefall in four hours. Not record time, but a whole lot faster than the seven hours it took us the first time, when Mark Tucker scolded us. I was happy with the time we made. That little bit of self-doubt I'd felt before was gone. Towards the top of the Icefall, the winds picked up and it got chillier. Normally, as you top out on the Icefall, it's an oven, so this wasn't bad. I actually enjoyed the climb up. Plus, climbing with Brien was a joy. He was always looking back, checking on my progress, and nodding his head and smiling as if to encourage me on.

Our plan was to spend one night at Camp 1. We were in no hurry because this was our major acclimatization foray. April 24 was my dad's birthday; he would have been 85. It was a hard day for me. I had lots of thoughts about him. I still missed him every day, but I was sure he was in a better place.

We were going to go up to Camp 2, but the weather had other plans for us. It was snowing heavily, the wind was blowing, and visibility was low. It would have been difficult avoiding the crevasses from Camp 1 to Camp 2.

Mark Tucker was at Camp 2, acclimatizing in case there was an emergency that demanded he climb higher. He was hoping to descend that day. Will, Brad, Jason, Mike, Mingma Ongel and Panuru were hoping to leave Base Camp to go to Camp 1. They radioed us to ask about the weather. We were giving them reports, but it was moot. There was an Icefall collapse above 19,000 feet; no one was going through there today. We started to climb up toward Camp 2, but after 10 minutes we turned back. There was just too much snow and too little visibility. Brien and I looked at each other and said, "What's the hurry?"

On April 25, we made our move to Camp 2 under more favorable conditions. It took us three hours to climb up from Camp 1—no big deal. Jason Tanguay had come up earlier that morning from Base Camp to join us for the climb up to Camp 2. It was nice to get into Advanced Base Camp and see the ABC cooks again.

The next day, we rested. But Will, Brad, Mike, Mingma Ongel and Panuru who were behind us at Camp 1, moved up to Camp 2 and Dan, Ron and Swee were on their way down from Camp 3, so we had a full house at Advanced Base Camp.

On April 27, there was some concern about the recent snow on the Lhotse Face. The angle of the face is fairly steep so the fresh snow usually sloughs off and falls. There was some debate about our moving up, but we deemed it reasonable to go. Camp 3 is at 24,000 feet, about two-thirds of the way up the Lhotse Face. It's a scary site chopped into the steep face. Tents have safety lines between them. You simply cannot slip up there. When Brien, Jason and I started up at 9 a.m. it was "Africa hot" and the combination of thin air and steepness conspired to make this a difficult and miserable ascent. When we reached our destination we decided we had earned an oxygen cocktail. We sucked some Os for 10 minutes. Tasty.

Brien and I shared a tent and Jason had his own tent. Our plan was to sleep that night without supplemental oxygen. After we did our chores, got snow to melt for water, and ate, we were ready to go to sleep. But it was only 7 p.m. It was pretty cold—zero to minus 10—and there the lack of oxygen makes sleep difficult. To know I was going to be in the sleeping bag from 7 p.m. to 7 a.m. didn't exactly thrill me. I slept very poorly, maybe three and one half hours. I was cold the entire night and I had a minor headache. Not fun, but part of the process.

Our plan on April 28 was to brew up, eat, and then climb above Camp 3 using supplemental oxygen. My goal was to refamiliarize myself with the system, go up higher and breathe oxygen. I hiked about two hours and deemed it a success.

That afternoon, Will, Brad and Mike arrived at Camp 3 with their Sherpas. Sherpas are smarter than us, which we knew. They don't sleep at Camps 1 and 3. They don't like Camp 3. "Why would you sleep there?" they always asked us, looking at the exposure. So, after they accompanied their climbers up they headed back down to ABC.

That night we slept with supplemental oxygen. I put on an oxygen mask at 6 p.m. and at 6:01, I was asleep. I woke up at midnight. I hadn't even moved. Sleeping was so much warmer because of having oxygen. I went back to sleep at 12:01. The next time I woke up it was 2 a.m. I'd already slept eight hours. I figured that was it for the night, that I wouldn't be able to sleep any more. Not so. I fell back asleep until 6 a.m. I slept 12 hours. That's unheard of, at least at that altitude, and I felt great.

The next day, refreshed from a full night's sleep, we descended easily to Camp 2. On April 30, we finished our foray with our hike back to Base Camp. Along the way we were delayed by a group from Adventure Consultants. Some of their members were moving super slow. They created a bit of a bottleneck at the top of the Icefall. I'm normally hard on myself for being so slow, but seeing those guys finally made me realize that I deserved to be here. I had often thought of myself as being the weakest, but obviously I wasn't.

The only setback from the descent was the sunburn I had gotten on my tongue. When you are breathing hard with your mouth open on a big mountain, you run the risk of getting your tongue sunburned. It's nasty. It hurts a lot. But after a bucket shower in Base Camp, I was feeling pretty good. It was time to wait for the proverbial window to open. As I wrote in my journal that day:

So now I've done all my acclimatization forays and I'm ready for our summit attempt after I get enough rest and if the weather is right.

LIFE AT THE KHUMBU COUNTRY CLUB

We would spend a good, solid week at Base Camp—resting, healing, and eating and drinking as much as possible—before making our summit bid. The waiting game had begun.

On May 1, we played Hillary Step. Willie Benegas, a transplanted Argentine from Berkeley, Calif., put in a route at the base of the Khumbu Icefall that was intended to mimic what the Hillary Step would be like for us on the Southeast Ridge. Willie was the main guide for Mountain Madness and was a big deal in mountaineering. Benegas and his twin brother, Damien, had put up some amazing routes in Patagonia and the previous spring climbed the incredibly difficult North Face of 25,790-foot Nuptse in Nepal. We tried to make our game of Hillary Step as realistic as possible—

strapping on oxygen masks and wearing goggles, gloves and our packs. The route wasn't super hard, but it was awkward. I thought it was a great exercise and very worthwhile.

By May 3, my sunburned tongue was healed. After a while, climbers become accustomed to always having some little problem. Most people get intestinal malaise and the Khumbu cough. The polite way to say it is nobody climbs the mountain healthy. The impolite way is the Everest creed: "Suffer fucker." In other words, you signed up for this, so you can't cry too much about it.

Don't get me wrong. It's not all suffering. Take May 5th, for instance. That was the day we played golf at the Khumbu Country Club. After breakfast, Mark Tucker went over to the Mountain Link camp and picked up his friend Jeff Justman, aka JJ. JJ and another guide, Craig Van Hoy, were climbing without clients. Originally, they arrived at Base Camp with three clients. One was a Taiwanese who spoke no English and was without the requisite skills to safely tackle the Big E. The other two were a couple who found out they were with child shortly after they arrived at Base Camp. By now, they had all gone home. So JJ had time for a little golf, too.

Tuck had packed a pitching wedge and 18 golf wiffle balls. We laid out a little course at the base of the Icefall. Legendary golf designer Robert Trent Jones would have been proud of us. The flat ice was used for fairways and ice formations provided elevated tees. We borrowed a porter's pack basket to make holes. We played golf for about two hours, laughing our butts off. I don't know what was a funnier sight, us playing golf at the base of the Khumbu Icefall or the Sherpas looking at us in utter amazement. I'm embarrassed to admit that JJ took the first annual Khumbu Open in a stunning upset—beating me—although he did have a nice swing. Tucker really didn't make the cut, but there was no cut—he came in last.

You do what you have to do for exercise. So we didn't take carts. In fact, we didn't even take Sherpas to be our caddies. We carried our own club.

A few days later, on May 8, I took a great hike toward Gorak Shep that ended up on top of 18,400-foot Kala Patar. I wanted to be by myself. I left Base Camp at 9:50 a.m. and as I was approaching Gorak Shep around 11 a.m., I cut up a trail toward Kala Patar. Kala Patar is about 1,250 feet above Gorak Shep. It was a beautiful morning and I was feeling good. I didn't run up Kala Patar, but I went up fast. I reached the top at noon. No one was there. No clouds. Everest was out in all its glory. A woman trekker arrived and took some photos of me. She was impressed that I was an Everest climber, but warned me to be careful up there. After a while, I hiked down to Gorak Shep and had lunch. I bought a couple bottles of Everest whiskey to take back to Base Camp. It costs 250 rupees for San Miguel beer or six ounces of Everest whiskey. (Same price, less weight, more alcohol, easy choice.) On my way back to camp, I was walking the ridgeline that goes above the Khumbu glacier and I realized there was a guy catching up to me. I didn't want to be passed, so I started walking faster. Finally, after a while, he motioned me to stop. He was gasping. "Wait, wait," he said. "Man, I can't keep up with you." I don't know why that made me feel good, but it did. I remembered thinking how much better I was feeling at that point than in 2002, when I was getting over Big Head Todd.

That night we relaxed in Base Camp. The Sherpas brought

in a case of beer, which was unusual. I had the Everest whiskey. We were all feeling pretty nutty. I felt like this was the calm before the storm. Jason and I were doing shots of whiskey out of our coffee cups. It was pretty crazy. We were feeling a little buzz, and then we started drinking beer. Brien was drinking beer and Dan was having some whiskey. It was a good time. Here we were at Everest Base Camp, laughing, telling stories and jokes, feeling pretty buzzed, knowing that we were about to have one of the hardest weeks of our lives.

ROCKIN' THROUGH THE ICEFALL

On May 9, it appeared that there would be a good weather window from May 14 to 17. You have to count your days backward to figure out when you should leave. We decided that Brien, Dan, Jason, Ron and I would start heading up on May 11. Four of us would be hanging together and Ron would be loosely attached, since he was a "solo" climber. We would work together as a team until High Camp. Then most of us would get the addition of a Sherpa for each man at a cost of $500 per person. That money went directly to the Sherpas.

The forecast on May 10 was good for the next day. In my journal, I wrote:

I plan to leave early tomorrow for Camp 2. Should be a

fairly long day. The plan is to go to C2 on 5/11, rest on 5/12, move to C3 on 5/13, up to High Camp on 5/14 and then go for the summit that night and hopefully top off during the a.m. of the 15th. I wouldn't be surprised if we wait an extra day at C2 for the route to get fixed. So maybe the 16th would be our summit bid. Who knows, just happy to get moving after hanging around BC for 10 days!

I remembered when Eric Simonson took our photo at Base Camp in the pre-dawn light on May 11, 2002. As we set out for our summit run I felt differently this time; I felt much better about making it. I still had that nagging Khumbu cough, but otherwise I was in good shape.

This was my third trip up through the Icefall. Brien, Dan and I started out together. Jason and Ron went ahead of us. They were climbing pretty fast. This was really the first time Dan and I had climbed together. Brien and I were always together because we'd gotten sick before the first foray. But Dan was a few days ahead of our schedule. Until now.

Dan and Brien, either consciously or subconsciously, made the right decision to put me in the lead. Dan clearly was the fastest and Brien was very strong as well. I was feeling strong, but by putting me in that position it increased my pace. You always push yourself just a little more when you know someone is behind you. I did that and we buzzed through the Icefall. From where you hit it to where you top out took us three hours. That was really good time. Before I'd felt like one of the weaker climbers on the mountain; I no longer felt that way. I felt really good to be teamed with these guys. It was unspoken, but it felt as if Jason, Dan and Brien were among the strongest, and I was keeping pace with them.

We topped out of the Icefall. Normally we would just stop at Camp 1 and rest for the night, but this time we were going all the way to Camp 2. I had been a little worried about going past Camp 1 on the first day, but I felt great when we got that far. I figured that going up the next three hours would be no big deal.

We got to Camp 2 in really good time, maybe seven hours total from Base Camp. I remember getting there and feeling great. You can't cheat acclimatization. Other times, you'd just get up there and feel dead. I remembered walking past those first dang tents and going and going and going up to our camp. It seemed to take forever. I felt good this time around. I knew the next day would be a rest day, and I was feeling good about that. I also knew that we were only just beginning.

If you break the mountain into pieces, moving from Base Camp to Camp 2 is the easy, low piece. The climbing, in my mind, really begins above Camp 2 on the Lhotse Face. You're higher and the climbing gets more desperate. Below Camp 2, you really don't deteriorate. Above Camp 2, you're going downhill physically. It's ironic. You're going downhill as you're going uphill.

TO CAMP 3

IMG's second group—Mike, Will, Brad and Swee, plus their Sherpas—were two days behind us. That was good. We didn't want to get in each other's way.

The weather up high was still a bit unsettled; there was no sign of that good-weather window yet. We were thinking we would be among the first to make an attempt at the summit, which is good and bad. The good side is that many teams hold back and wait for the route to be put in, so it would be less crowded when we went for the top. The risky part is we didn't know what the snow conditions would be up high. If it were really deep, it would take a lot of effort to kick in steps. Plus, the route up high would need to be fixed. We were hoping the Sherpas would be able to fix lines from High Camp to the Balcony—from 26,200 to 27,500 feet—on May 14. Then the plan was to have the stronger Sherpas head up first, in front of us, to fix the last bit of the route. That's always problematic. Snow conditions and timing have to be just right. Of course, the weather plays a part and communication can be a problem. One year, on the first day that teams were attempting the summit, the Sherpas fixed to the South Summit in places that didn't need to be fixed, and ran out of rope up high. Everyone had to turn around, just 300 vertical feet short of the summit.

Going to Camp 3 is steep and there were still concerns about the weather when we set out the morning of May 13. But two-thirds of the way from Camp 2 to Camp 3, I was feeling great. I reminded myself that this was my last trip up, which always feels good. I was going up over ground I wouldn't need to ascend again. We were sailing up there. It was clear, but windy—20 to 30 mph, not awful. Up high we could see the wind was ripping. Every step was bringing us closer to Camp 3 and I was thinking, "This is cake." Then, all of a sudden, the walkie-talkies went off. Climbers ahead of us were spinning. I couldn't believe they were turning around. Mark Tucker was wondering from Base Camp if we should turn around and return to Camp 2. I saw David Breashears and his Sherpas turn around up ahead of us. I was thinking, "Do they know something we don't know?" I figured we were going to turn around and I was pretty bummed out.

Dorje Llama called from Camp 4 and said the weather wasn't that bad. I was encouraged, but nervous. I didn't want to give up the ground we had gained. But I also didn't want to get above Advanced Base Camp (Camp 2) and get stuck, where it was possible we would deteriorate physically while we waited out bad weather.

We went up anyway. When we reached Camp 3, I was sharing a tent with my buddy Brien. He made it up there ahead of me and had everything ready to go. He had gathered snow for everyone to melt for water. That's Brien.

Everything takes longer up high. We had to melt a lot of snow for a little drinking water and the thinner air made the melting process a time-consuming project.

We had decent weather. It was windy, but the sun was out, so inside the tent was warm. Tents up higher are smaller. It was super cramped with two people and oxygen bottles.

After we settled in and got hydrated, we went to visit Jason and Dan's tent. Four men cramped into a tent not really big enough for two people. Why? To play Hearts, of course. This was a good sign; we were not beat up. We were yelling, cursing and screaming at each other, having fun—as usual. Ron was alone in his tent. The solo climber. He didn't play our reindeer games.

In my journal, I wrote:

Now it's time to get serious. It's important to get ahead of the hydration, food and sleep curve. In 2002, I felt bad going from C3 to C4 and blew my chance at the summit.

Camp 3 would be our last chance for a reasonable night's sleep before our summit attempt. Eating and drinking as much as possible here would pay dividends up higher.

The last time, my move from Camp 3 to Camp 4 was where everything unraveled for me. I'd been thinking about this for nearly the last two years. This time I slept well, on oxygen, at Camp 3. It was a good start.

CAMP 3 TO CAMP 4

It was a little windy the night of May 13. We were wondering, "Do we spend an extra night at Camp 3, waiting for the weather to be better and the route to be fixed? Do we go up or even do we go down?"

I woke up at 5 a.m. on May 14 to Jason talking to Tuck on the walkie-talkie. It sounded like all systems go. It was time to get to work. We were moving with a purpose. Every second, every minute would really count from here on up. If we were headed up, I wanted to get hydrated, eat, strap on my oxygen and get going to the South Col so I'd be prepared for my summit attempt.

I was the first one from our group on the route, starting at 6:35 a.m. I made good progress. I was setting a good pace, sucking on three liters of oxygen per minute. All the mystery of climbing from Camp 3 to Camp 4 was gone. The weather was a bit cold and windy. The skies were clear and we were in the shade since the sun wasn't above the surrounding mountains yet. But I was in my baffled down suit and warm. I worried that when the sun came out I'd overheat. In 2002, I broiled.

Ron and Brien caught up to me at the Yellow Band, high up the Lhotse Face at about 25,000 feet. The Yellow Band was difficult climbing. It was steep, angled at about 40 or 45 degrees. But what made it most difficult was that it was a series of overhanging slabs, best described as something like enormous roofing tiles. You climb over these slippery, snow-covered slabs in clunky boots and crampons. There were fixed lines all over the place, left behind by previous expeditions. I tried to find the newest looking fixed line and placed my ascender on it. Then I'd clip my safety carabiner into another line as a backup. It wasn't super hard climbing, just uncomfortable. Spikes on rock. If you were to fall here, and the fixed line failed to hold, well, it would be a fall that would not be stoppable.

The last time I climbed over the Yellow Band, I turned my oxygen down and by the time I reached the top of the band I was knackered. This time, I kept the Os flowing and I felt good. It was work, but I was doing OK.

At the top of the Yellow Band, I took a water break with Brien, Jason and Dan. The weather was chilly, probably below zero, but we were in the sun now so the temperature in my baffled down suit felt just about right. It was cold enough to keep me from overheating.

We reached the Geneva Spur; a distinctive rock rib below the South Col. This was mixed ice and rock climbing and the upper part of the spur was pretty steep. Brien and Jason moved ahead of Dan and me. We were all doing fine. In 2002, when I got to the top of the spur, I was alone, tired and spent. This time, I was with Dan. When I got to the top, I still had energy in reserve. From there, it was an easy 20-minute stroll to Camp 4. It was a nice stroll, a far cry from the slog I struggled to finish in 2002. I'm sure Dan could have gone faster, but we were hanging together. We pulled into the South Col at 1:30 p.m. In 2002, I hadn't arrived there until after 4 p.m. Two years earlier, I knew my climb was done. Not so this time around.

In my journal, I wrote:

I wasn't sure if I'd make the summit, but I damn sure was going to get out of the tent to give it a try.

COUNTDOWN AT HIGH CAMP

Seven and one half hours and counting. We arrived at High Camp at 1:30 p.m. and at 9 p.m. that night we would start to get ready for our summit bid. Seven and one half hours and counting.

Once we got to Camp 4 (or High Camp), it was a funny kind of day. We had already made a pretty big climb from about 24,000 to 26,200 feet, but we were far from done. Instead of resting on our laurels, we tried to get some rest—eat, hydrate, and prepare for the night ahead.

We wanted to get to sleep at 5 or 6 p.m. and hoped to get three hours of sleep. That would be a big bonus. At 9 p.m., when it's pitch-black, you start to get ready to go. It's nice to be moving by 10:30 p.m. So when you should be your strongest, you're sleep deprived. You've jammed two days of climbing into one. Everything you've been doing since you started trekking in prepares you for the most important 24 hours of this climb. Everything is a pyramid. It had been 52 days for us to this point. Acclimatizing, staying healthy, staying mentally focused—and this was what it all boiled down to. The clock was speeding up as you headed for the summit. You found yourself thinking, "Where'd the time go?"

There we were, right at the doorstep. But this time I was psyched to be there. I was with my buds. The last time was my Roberto Duran *"no mas"* thing. This time I knew I was going to get out of the tent. I knew I had a chance at it.

I was assigned a tent with Dan and Ron. Ron complained about me being with him because he thought I might snore. I wasn't happy about this and neither was Jason, who made up the tent assignments. When Ron realized we wouldn't be sleeping much anyway he let it go. Dan slept between us.

Jason and Brien shared the other tent. I had shot a lot of video up until that point. I decided I was not going to carry the video camera on summit day. It would have been nice, but I didn't need the extra weight. I was just focused on climbing.

But I remembered the 2002 video I'd shot after arriving in High Camp. I was shooting out of the tent's vestibule, showing the route the others would end up taking to the summit. I remembered how my voice sounded: I was a beaten man. You could hear in my voice that it was game over. I was barely able to talk. You could hear the depression, exhaustion and tears as I spoke. This time, I shot the same scene. But now I was this happy little camper. My narration even made sense. I was speaking in complete sentences, not affected by the altitude. I sounded focused, determined and upbeat. Not getting out of the tent in 2002 had haunted me. I'd had to live with it for the previous 728 days, but who was counting. I was pretty excited about putting that behind me.

Dan was his normal upbeat self. "Hey, *compadre*," he said with a big grin, "what do you think? We're on the doorstep."

The tent was crowded. We were all trying to put layers on, discussing what we were going to wear and take. I brought fresh socks—two big, heavy pair—that would be my summit socks. I debated with myself, "Should I sleep in one pair; what if I sweat?" I put the inner booties from my double-plastic climbing boots inside the sleeping bag to keep them warm. In the nighttime up high we knew it would be well below zero. I didn't have a thermometer. People always asked me how cold did it get up there. I don't know what the temperature was, but it was cold. Damn cold.

By 4:45 p.m. we were ready to try to get some sleep. Jason brought around the Sherpas who would be climbing with each of us. They weren't there to guide, just to stay with us and help if we needed it. "These are great people to have by your side at the most difficult time," Simonson had told us.

I was assigned Mingma Tshering, the Sherpa who had trained to be a Buddhist monk and who had helped with our Puja at the beginning of the climb. He was really quiet, very shy. He didn't speak much English. While I got to know quite a few of the Sherpas as we climbed, he was sort of in the background. He was always smiling and friendly, but I didn't really know him.

The Sherpas would carry our extra oxygen bottle. Our bottles were the big heavy ones. When filled, they weighed about 17 pounds. But at three liters per minute, you had 10 hours of oxygen. We figured two bottles for the climb to the top and back to High Camp. At three liters per minute, I had 20 hours. If it takes more than 20 hours, it's way too long. The Sherpas only use one bottle on summit day and use a lower oxygen flow rate.

Most expeditions use the Russian-made Poisk oxygen bottles. They're much lighter but also hold less oxygen. Consequently, those climbers needed four or five Poisk bottles for their summit day.

The Sherpas would carry our extra bottle and drop it at the Balcony, up at 27,500 feet. We would change bottles there. The bottle we started out with would be half gone. We would put on a full bottle to get to the summit and back to the Balcony. Then we would switch again and finish the descent. We figured that this would work out just fine—for most people.

Brien, Dan and Jason also had a Sherpa. Ron had declined because he thought of himself as a solo climber.

There were a couple of expeditions at High Camp with us—teams from Chile and Greece. The other IMG climbers were now at Camp 2. They would move from Camp 2 to Camp 3 when we were going for the summit. Then, when we moved down from Camp 4 to Camp 2, they would move in to occupy High Camp.

The wind was flapping the tent loudly as we lay in our sleeping bags, trying to get some sleep. We were so full of anticipation. Any kind of sleep we could get would be a bonus. I knew this, which probably made going to sleep even more difficult. I was amazed because at some point I actually did fall asleep. We were awakened at 9 p.m. and told to get ready.

However, the wind was still blowing and we would have to wait until 11 p.m. to make the go/no-go decision.

WINDY CITY

To go or not to go. That was the question. I've thought a lot about the go/no-go decision. In mountaineering, it is pretty obvious—usually. There are times you want to go, like my time on Denali when I spent a week at High Camp, chomping at the bit. I wanted to go, but, obviously, not going was the right decision. The weather never cooperated. Now, if you waited for conditions to be absolutely perfect, you would never go. You do have to accept some risk. But the summit-at-all-costs mentality is wrong. In that case, you'll go, but you may not return. The summit was only the halfway point; it wasn't the final destination.

As I've mentioned before, many of the same principles applied to flying and to business. As an instrument-rated pilot who flies in the clouds, I accepted some risk. The gist is, I have to be well-rested, focused and on top of my game. In addition to that, I have to think, "Is my airplane safe?" One of the biggies, when it comes to deciding to go as a pilot, is the weather. Is it good enough to go? You can't make stupid decisions. Don't suffer from get-there-itis. It's not get-home-at-all-costs. That's very much like the summit-at-all-cost attitude. Takeoff was always optional, but landing was mandatory. You were going to come down. If you were going to launch yourself, you better make damn sure you could come down safely. There are many parallels between flying and climbing. While mountaineering is more physically demanding, flying in the clouds is one of the toughest things I do mentally.

Business decisions might not be life and death, but they can be the difference between success and failure. You don't get ahead without taking some risk. You make decisions without knowing with certainty what is going to happen.

On the night of May 14, it was windy but clear. We hemmed and hawed about what to do. Two years before, I would have loved for that to have happened. I know what I would have said then, "Wait, wait." That would have bought me time to make a summit attempt. But this time was different. I was anxious and ready to go. I couldn't wait to get out of the tent. That was my psychological barrier. I kept thinking, "What happens if we have to wait another day?" The weather was supposed to be good, but you never know.

It was a starry night outside the tent. Finally at 11 o'clock, after a fair amount of deliberation, a decision was made. Tucker and Jason were the ones who made the call with input from the rest of the group. We were pretty fat on oxygen so we knew it wasn't a desperate situation. We weren't painted into a corner. We could have hung out at High Camp, slept another day, and gone up. The bummer about that was, even though we would have been able to sleep, our bodies would have been deteriorating. We were in the Death Zone; a harsh environment where your body is literally dying. Because we had input on the decision, I was definitely for going.

Tucker told us, "It's not uncommon for winds to start out breezy and diminish through the night. The forecast for tomorrow is good."

Let's go.

OUT OF THE TENT

As soon as we woke up at 9 that night, I was surprised. I remembered hearing the Sherpas unzipping our tent. I nearly jumped. "Where am I?!" I thought.

Within a second, I was kicking into gear. "Oh, yeah, it's summit day. Hot damn."

So the scurrying began. It was summit day. I told myself, "You've done this before. Not on Everest, but on Rainier, Kilimanjaro, Aconcagua, McKinley." It was time to get organized. All systems were go.

When you climb, you break summit day into little tasks. First, I needed to get my act together and get out of the tent in a timely manner. Time really does accelerate. Even though it was going to be a long day, it's amazing how a long day can go by really fast. I wanted to take advantage of every minute.

As we were getting ready, waiting on the decision to go or not to go, we knew it was important to get hydrated. I took two liters of water and a couple thousand calories in candy bars, Cliff bars and other energy stuff. You should drink more than two liters of water, but I didn't want to carry more than two. So I needed to hydrate as much as possible before leaving the tent. I ate oatmeal, some candy bars and Gu before leaving. I tried to get as many calories in me as possible. I knew it was going to be a big day and I wasn't going to be eating much after this.

Even though we didn't know if we were going yet, we got our gear on and got ready to go.

I wore lightweight long underwear, expedition-weight underwear, fleece bibs, a couple fleece layers on top and then my baffled down suit. I had my good-luck reindeer copulation hat from Ersh, of course. I also had a balaclava with me to use as a neck gaiter. I wore ice-climbing gloves and threw fleece mitts and overmitts into my pack in case it got really cold. On my feet, I had a light pair of polypro socks and two pairs of thick mountaineering socks under my Everest OneSport boots. I would also wear crampons on my feet. My boots were roomy. You wanted the boots to fit, but you wanted enough room for circulation to prevent frostbite. I would wear UV-protected goggles and carry a pair of glacier glasses as a backup. The goggles would provide warmth for my eyeballs. I debated about whether to wear them, but I remembered that Phil had frozen his eyeballs in 2001. Plus, it was windy. I would carry a spare headlamp with fresh batteries because I felt it would be easier to switch the entire headlamp rather than changing a battery or a bulb up high. Everyone carried his or her own walkie-talkie and I had a thermos to keep water from freezing.

When I looked outside the tent there was a mixture of excitement, anticipation and trepidation. This was the beginning of the longest day of my life. I was hoping it would go well. There were not as many other teams at High Camp as we thought there would be. That raised some concerns—for our own strength, the weather and the route. We wondered if there would be enough Sherpas to fix the lines up high. But we were excited when the decision was finally made to go.

At 11 p.m., I got out of the tent. I remembered a quote from Marv Levy, the Hall of Fame Football Coach of the Buffalo Bills. During the team huddle, just prior to the kickoff of every game, he would say, "Where else would you rather be than right here, right now?!" That's how I felt.

The Sherpas were mingling around us, sort of impatient. You could tell they were thinking, "Let's get going." I put my spikes on and was ready to go. After using your crampons so much, it was second nature to put them on. You snapped in and you knew by the sound that it was on correctly.

Away we went. There was no group photo, no group hug. There was just this amazing focus on getting moving. I think we all had a sense of urgency. "A let's take advantage of all the time we have mentality." I was a little disappointed that the weather had cost us 40 minutes. Our original plan was to start at 10:30 p.m., but we started at 11:10 p.m.

IT ALL STARTED OUT SO WELL

There were nine of us headed for the summit: Jason with his Sherpa, Panuru; Brien with Karma Rita; Dan with Tashi Dorje; Ron climbing "solo;" and me with Mingma Tshering.

The Sherpas were carrying two bottles of oxygen. They would use one bottle for themselves all day at a lower flow rate than we used. The other one they lugged up the mountain was our second bottle.

Once we started out, we were in a small world defined by how far our headlamp could go. We were moving in slow motion up the triangular face heading toward the Southeast Ridge. The wind calmed down a little bit, but it was still breezy.

My Sherpa Mingma started leaving the Col quickly.

He ran away from High Camp. At least it felt as if he were running. We were on rocky, flat ground at first. But even on that terrain, I knew it was a pace I could not maintain. I knew we had to move fast, but I was thinking, "I hope this isn't the pace he's expecting me to keep."

Finally, Mingma let me set the pace. I needed to find a pace that would work for me. I wanted to be consistent. I didn't want to take lots of rest breaks. Be steady. Don't go too fast or too slow. Put your body on autopilot. Step, breathe, breathe. Let your mind daydream. Step, breathe, breathe. Pay attention to the climbing, but don't think too much about how the body is feeling. Step, breathe, breathe. My most successful climbs felt like out-of-body experiences. Step, breathe, breathe.

There was always something about climbing at night that added scariness, desperation and even wonderment. There were shooting stars and heat lightning over Tibet. It was amazing to see. I wondered if everyone was seeing it, but I didn't really have the energy or shouting ability to say, "Hey, look at that." I stayed quiet within myself in my own little world. Step, breathe, breathe.

About one and one half hours after we set out, Tashi Dorje became ill. He had lower GI problems, a case of "the squirts." Someone caught up to Mingma and explained the situation. Mingma was given Dan's extra bottle of oxygen; the one Tashi Dorje would have carried. That meant he was carrying three oxygen bottles and his backpack probably weighed around 60 pounds. Apparently that was no big deal for Mingma. Stopping and waiting for this situation to sort itself out probably cost us about half an hour. Time was precious. Oxygen was precious.

When we stopped, my toes got a little cold. I wanted to keep moving, but I knew this wasn't a good situation. It underscored that while the Sherpas are super strong, they were human beings and they could get sick, too. Tashi Dorje went back down to High Camp.

And then there were eight.

We had crossed the rocky part of the South Col, then icy sections, crevasses and then the steep snow slope of the triangular face. It was easy going, but steep. Pretty straightforward climbing and well-fixed. Up we went. Step, breathe, breathe.

Everything started to get a little confusing to me after this. People who read *Into Thin Air* ask, "Why didn't they do this or do that?" Communication is problematic. Just identifying the climber next to you can be difficult. Truth be told, I wasn't even aware that Mingma was carrying Dan's extra bottle of oxygen until days later.

There was snow and rock above 27,000 feet. It was harder going. The climbing would get more difficult yet as we ascended through the night. The hours melted away. The route was fixed pretty well. I could see some headlamps at the Balcony. It was around 4:30 a.m. The pre-dawn light was just barely perceptible. We weren't far from gaining the Ridge. Somewhere, Dan looked around and caught some sort of reflection. He told me later that he figured it was the body of Scott Fischer, a famous guide who perished in 1996. A little creepy. No, a lot creepy. I was glad I didn't see him.

There was a lot more rock than I thought there would be up high. About 100 to 200 vertical feet below the Balcony was a steep snowfield. There was no fixed line. It wasn't a huge deal. It was just about dawn. We reached the Balcony around

5 a.m. It was still pretty cold but the wind, as predicted, was gone.

The Balcony was the start of the true Southeast Ridge. We were treated to a beautiful view of Makalu as the sun was rising with those tremendous long rays. The light was beautiful. Makalu is the fifth highest mountain in the world and we were now roughly level with its summit. As soon as the sun came up, it got a little warmer.

When we reached the Balcony, I felt good. In control. I still felt like myself. I was very aware and cognizant. My cough was still bothering me, but otherwise I was OK. Dan and I were the last to reach the Balcony. It was a fabulous morning. We had a bite to eat, drank some water, and strapped on a fresh bottle of oxygen. There was some talking going on, but I wasn't totally paying attention. The wind was a whisper at this point. The Balcony was an exquisite place to view the Himalaya. There was a layer of clouds about 15,000 feet below us. It was stunning. I had to pinch myself. "Holy, crap, I'm on Mount Everest. We're doing this. And I DID get out of that damn tent at High Camp."

A COUPLE OF LITTLE THINGS GO WRONG

We'd had a bit of a slow start and a delay, but we made reasonable time getting to the Balcony. It was going. I wasn't looking far enough ahead to think about whether I'd make the summit or not but we were halfway there. The easy half. From here, I figured I'd be up in five or six hours and back down to the balcony in three hours.

We sat on a little plateau, taking a rest. It lasted longer than I thought it should—maybe 30 to 40 minutes. There was a problem of which I was unaware. Panuru had a leaky oxygen bottle. He had realized that his bottle was nearly empty. That left us short an oxygen bottle. It was deemed that Jason would lose his Sherpa. Panuru would go down.

We'd already lost Tashi Dorje, who had gotten sick. Now we were losing another Sherpa.

And then there were seven.

Even though it was happening 20 feet away from me, I was unaware that this was going on. I was in my own little world.

Little did I know things were conspiring against us. Not only were we losing another one of our Sherpas, but a couple of other teams in High Camp that had said they were going to go for the summit and provide Sherpa support had never left their tents. They ended up going the next day. We were concerned about the fixing of lines above us.

On everestnews.com, Simonson reported:

Just heard from Mark Tucker at Base Camp on the sat phone at 7:15 am Nepal time. He says the IMG climbers are above the Balcony, but below the South Summit, in a part of the climb which has difficult communication to Base Camp because they are on the back side of the SE Ridge for a ways. Last report was that the Chileans are in front and IMG behind them. The weather is reported to be very nice. It sounds like a number of the teams that were planning to go today and assist with the rope fixing decided at the last minute not to go, so there are not many climbers up there. This is good—no traffic jam problems—but it sure would be nice to have some more horsepower up there for route work and fixing. Keep your fingers crossed!

– Eric Simonson, IMG Expeditions

MY WATCH SAYS 10:30 A.M. ALREADY

I didn't understand what was going on. I just wanted to get going. It was a perfect day. The view from the Balcony was killer. It was just stunning. The photograph I took here was the best photo I'd ever taken.

Finally, we started up again. Unbeknownst to me was the whole Panuru oxygen debacle and the trouble with the fixed lines. Jason had gone on ahead to speak to the Greeks and Chileans. I didn't know it, but we had been waiting for him to come back from talking to them. He told us the Greeks weren't even planning to fix lines. They were going to rope up, which wasn't usually done on Everest. If one falls, everyone falls.

I was starting to think, "Did we screw up? Did we have get-there-itis? Should we have waited another day?"

We ascended an unroped section to about 27,800 feet. It wasn't that hard, but at nearly 28,000 feet we were breathing heavily while sucking on oxygen. Everything was a little harder at 28,000 feet. I was on autopilot when it came to considering danger. I remember thinking, "That's it. I'm done." While this unroped section wasn't too bad, I couldn't accept the risk of climbing higher through unfixed sections that would be much steeper. It was a no-brainer for me. I was going to turn around and I didn't even feel that badly about it. I'd gotten out of the tent. I was about 98 percent sure I was turning back. A lack of fixed lines meant a lack of a safety net—too much risk for me.

"Take a deep breath and slow down," Jason said. "The weather is perfect."

He was right. We couldn't have asked for a nicer day. If the weather had been the least bit iffy, I think we would have spun right there. But we were able to stop and take another break to consider our options.

Karma Rita volunteered to go up with a Sherpa from another group to pull out old fixed lines and put in some new ropes where necessary. Slowly, but surely, I was thinking maybe I would go. Dan was going. Brien was thinking about it. I had some time to mull this over.

We waited for close to 90 minutes. It took a while. Karma Rita reported back that it was good to go. I was concerned because time just kept slipping through our fingers. But we decided as a group, "Let's go up and see how it goes. Everyone can make their own decision from there."

I felt pretty good along the ridge. It was straightforward except for some rocky areas I needed to climb over. I was trying to do the mental gymnastics to figure out my oxygen.

I was thinking everything was OK. We were above 28,000 feet and gaining on it, slowly. We were about as high as K2, the second-highest mountain in the world. It was incredible to be that high.

As I looked up, there were several false summits leading to the South Summit, so it was hard to tell where we were on the mountain. I knew from the South Summit you could see the true summit. But not from where we were, which made it difficult. Then my mind started playing tricks on me. I was still climbing OK and I was in touch with my whole group. I was coughing occasionally, but I felt mentally fit. Or so I thought.

That's when I checked my watch and it said 10:30 a.m. Not good. At best, it would take one and one half hours to get to the South Summit. They say it takes two to three hours roundtrip to go from there to the true summit and then back to the South Summit. I figured, "Let's say three hours for me because I'm slower than the rest. That's late. That's the edge of the limit for my bottle of oxygen." I thought, "This is bad."

I kept climbing, but in my mind I knew the timing was wrong. I asked Jason if he thought it was going to be OK.

"We're fine," he said, which surprised me because he usually was conservative.

I turned to Mingma. He was holding fixed lines to keep them taut for me. I asked him if we had enough time to get to the summit and back.

"Sure," he said, "it's not a problem."

He thought we had time, too. I felt that all of this was odd. I looked at my watch again. Probably about 10 minutes had passed since I looked at it before. But it still said 10:30 a.m.

In my journal, I wrote:

I check my altimeter/watch again and it's still 10.30. Except I'm an idiot. 10.30 is the barometric pressure, not the time. It's really only 8:07 a.m. And for the first time I think we might climb this mother.

My Suunto watch had three settings: altitude, barometric pressure and time. The altitude is measured by barometric pressure. It normally reads around 29.92 at sea level. At the altitude we were at, it read 10.30. Up high, the barometric pressure is incredibly low, which shows you how little oxygen there is, about one third as much available oxygen versus sea level. Of course we were using supplemental oxygen, sucking the sweet gas. But breathing supplemental Os doesn't simulate being at sea level. In reality, it's like being only three or four thousand feet lower.

Now I had to laugh at myself. I also had to start believing we were really going to climb to the top. We were going to make it.

SOUTH SUMMIT

I think the others pulled ahead at this point. I was starting to feel a little tired. I arrived at the South Summit with only Mingma. The rest of the group was 30 to 45 minutes ahead of me. On other mountains this might be unusual. But on Everest we were self-guided. We were on our own.

I probably didn't make the South Summit until almost 11:30 a.m. I don't know where all the time went. I was coughing more and starting to think that this was taking a lot out of me. But that's not unnatural. The going up part is tough. Coming down, with the aid of gravity—hopefully not too much, too quickly—would be okay. I was convinced of that.

We'd been going for 12 hours by this time. In my original grand plan I'd hoped to be to the summit by now and on my way back down. But we had wasted so much time—40 minutes at the beginning, 30 minutes for Tashi Dorje, 30 minutes at the Balcony, 90 minutes making our decision regarding fixed lines. We had lost more than three hours. Even with rest breaks, without all that lost time I would have been at the South Summit at 9:30 a.m. That would have been pretty good.

But now I was starting to question whether I could get to the summit and back in time. I didn't have a turn-around time. The 2 p.m. time was always bandied about, so that was in my head. I'd wanted to make it to the summit before noon—and that wasn't going to happen.

Simo calls the South Summit:

The most spectacular little piece of real estate that I can imagine. Below are the Col, the Cwm, and all of the Khumbu. Above is the Traverse to the Summit and the Hillary Step. The Southwest Face is at your feet. Off to the side are the Kangschung Face and Tibet. Makalu and Lhotse are a stone's throw away. The Traverse and the Hillary Step are steep and intimidating. They need to be fixed and it is critical that this be accomplished before the climbers reach the South Summit. This is the crux of the climb, both going up and down.

The freakiest part was looking at that knife's-edge ridge. It was the highest I'd ever been—28,750 feet, pretty gosh-darn high—and what I was about to do was not a cakewalk.

I'd heard of folks who'd made it to the South Summit, but didn't go to the true summit and I'd always thought, "It's only about 280 vertical feet. How in the world can you be that close and not finish?" I was about to find out.

TRUE SUMMIT

I descended 40 or 60 vertical feet down to that knife-edge ridge. The climbing had been pretty straightforward and then, all of a sudden, it was exposed. Big time. It was 10,000 feet down to Tibet on my right and 8,000 feet down to Nepal on my left.

I knew it was late, but it never occurred to me to stop. I was in a semi-hypnotic state, "Must ... get ... to ... summit." Step, breathe, breathe, breathe, breathe.

It was easy to get down to the traverse to the summit. But then, there was less snow and more sloped, exposed rock than I expected. I remember at one point I slipped and fell. I was on the fixed lines. Without those fixed lines I might not have stopped. It would have been a quick trip down into Nepal. That was jarring. It was the first time I'd slipped in a place where I shouldn't. I was never really scared. It was not one of those moments where your heart comes up into your throat. It was more of a dull, "I slipped—that was bad."

I was moving in slow motion, breathing the Os, in my own little world. Step, breathe, breathe, breathe, breathe. Everyone had gone ahead. No one made world-record time going up. Maybe that was because they were fixing the route still. But they were all far ahead of me. And my slow pace was now getting slower.

I made it across the traverse and reached the famed Hillary Step, the last significant obstacle before the summit. The weather was holding up great and I was feeling fair at best. I was a little shaken from that slip and in the back of my mind I knew it was getting late and I'd been pushing my oxygen reserves. But I couldn't will myself to go any faster. At some point Jason passed me. He was on his way down. As he went by he said, "Hey, man, it's getting kind of late, be careful." He wouldn't tell me to turn around because we were unguided. But that was his way of warning me.

There was no bottleneck at the Hillary Step. There were about 15 lines hanging there. I knew which one to take. It was easier going up the Hillary Step than I imagined. Slow, but relatively easy.

I'd always heard it was a simple stroll to the top once you'd gotten above the Hillary Step. I thought I'd be close. I was thinking five or ten minutes more. But I saw people around the true summit and they didn't look that close. I figured it was closing on 2 o'clock. "Where did the time melt away?"

I didn't have a firm grasp on the time, but I knew we were late. The rational voice in my head was saying, "You should spin this. You should turn around."

I said to Mingma, "How much further to the top?"

He was very encouraging. "Only ten more minutes."

I thought, "Only ten minutes. I can't turn around." In my trance, I continued plodding. At sea level it would have taken three or four minutes, tops. Mingma's assurance that it was ten minutes took me 30 minutes. I was feeling drained.

I remembered seeing a cornice to my right and thinking, "That's really airy over there. Don't walk too close to that— if you break through you might keep going." I concentrated on the placement of my boots. I had tunnel vision. I don't remember soaking in the view. It was more like a trail of tears. I had to rest quite frequently. Step, breathe, breathe, breathe, breathe. I was coughing, but that was something that I thought was normal. I was gassed, but everyone was gassed on Mount Everest.

I looked ahead. Mingma was standing on top. He'd gone ahead of me. There was a metal pole with a boatload of prayer flags. The true summit, the Holy Grail. But between Mingma and me were another 20 vertical feet. Step, breathe, breathe, breathe, breathe. Finally, with five or six steps to go, I powered up and took those steps without a rest break.

I turned around and sat down on the summit. It was 2:20 in the afternoon. I had reached the rooftop of the world.

I felt no joy once I reached the summit. No joy whatsoever. Just a profound sense of relief that I could now turn around and go down.

It was not like the anticipation of getting to a summit on any mountain I had climbed before. I always got that last bit of adrenaline and excitement. I remembered climbing to the summit of McKinley with tears in my eyes and joy inside, feeling as if my heart was going to burst with joy. I stood tall for the big hero shot on top.

That didn't happen on Everest. I plodded to the top, sat down, and dully thought about having to get back down.

Mingma and I were the last two of 21 to make the pretty well defined summit of Everest on the first day that anyone had gotten up in 2004. There were so many things that I wanted to say and do. All I could do was snap a few photos. I didn't even take scenery photos. I had Mingma take two photos of me and I took one of him.

People would ask me, "What's it like to stand on the summit of Everest?" I wouldn't know. When I got to the top, I sat down.

You think about that moment of victory. Of course, the real moment of victory is when you return from the summit to Base Camp safely. But I had been wanting to bring my video camera up with me. When Ershler reminded me to remember why I was up there, I figured the extra one and one half pounds weren't worth it. I wanted video footage and beautiful panoramic photos. I'd thought of putting my helmet cam on for the traverse and Hillary Step. I wanted to record special greetings—how much I appreciated Maggie's support. I'd be spewing profundities left and right. I wanted to thank my business partners, family and friends for this moment. I wanted to stand there and hold up my ice ax proudly in the classic hero mountaineer pose. All I could do was sit on the summit and pose for a summit photo in which I wasn't even smiling. It was grim.

I spent five or ten minutes on top of the world, feeling anything but. I never even took a sweeping look around. I'd wanted to look down at the route on the North Side. I didn't.

I'd always thought about how cool and fun it would be to be on the summit of Mount Everest. It was none of that for me. All I knew was I had a very long descent ahead of me and I was exhausted. I also knew my oxygen was getting dangerously low.

It was 2:30. It was going to be dark in four or five hours. I figured I had less than two hours of oxygen. I didn't know exactly when it would run out, but I knew it was going to be close. It would probably run out before getting back to my other bottle, stashed below at the Balcony.

On descent, I'm usually pretty good. People who don't climb think that making the summit is when the hard work is done. But going down is when you have to be cautious. Think about climbing the stairs: going up, if you trip it's not that big a deal, but if you trip when you're going down, you fall. Most accidents occur on descent, when you're tired. I knew I didn't want to be one of those. But I wasn't really alarmed by this thought. I should have been, but everything just felt dull.

I'LL JUST BIVY HERE

I realized as I started heading down that I felt like crap. The plug had been pulled. I was woefully, physically inadequate for the task ahead of me. Panic began to set in. But again it was a dull panic. All the edges were taken off. I knew, rationally, that it was bad to feel this bad and for my oxygen to be this low.

Slowly, Mingma and I made our way down to the top of the Hillary Step. It was a two-section rappel. For most of the fixed lines I would arm rappel, wrapping the rope around my arms and sliding down. The Hillary Step was pretty steep so I decided to rappel it using my mechanical belay/rappel device. I rappelled the first section without any problem. Then, as I rappelled the second part and was almost down, I placed my foot at the base of the Hillary Step and slipped.

I did a 180. Suddenly, my head was down below my feet, ass over teakettle. There were all those lines hanging there and I got tangled up in them. I had a 30-pound backpack hanging up toward my head, making me top heavy. It was a pretty desperate situation. I tried to right myself, but I was so weak I couldn't do it. Normally, this wouldn't be a problem. But I was upside-down, like a fly trapped in a spider web on the Hillary Step on Mount Everest.

I was panting, completely out of breath, freaked out. Dully, I thought, "This isn't good."

But before I could make another attempt in earnest to get out of this trap, Mingma was there, by my side, righting my wrong. He grabbed hold and helped untangle me. I think he had to cut a rope or two to get me out of the mess.

When I was free, I had to sit down and regain my composure. Mingma was looking at me pleadingly.

"We must go," he said.

I'm not sure I could have gotten out of that mess without someone there. Maybe. Maybe not. That little episode took a lot out of me.

After that, I made the traverse without incident. Except that I needed to rest frequently. I was moving painfully slow.

We reached the col between the true summit and the South Summit and I looked up. The 60-foot climb back up to the South Summit seemed insurmountable. I looked at Mingma, who was standing there waiting for me.

"I can't go on," I told him. "I'm going to bivy here."

People have tried to bivouac (overnight without shelter) that high on Everest before and a few survived. Most didn't. And those who made it usually ended up with fewer toes and fingers. So it was not advisable. Not by any stretch of the imagination.

I called Mark Tucker at Base Camp and told him what was going on. I was thinking there was no way I could go on. I was really shaken by my fall. I was mad I'd fallen twice. I was thinking, "If I just rest here for the night, I'll be better."

"Do you have any medications with you?" Tuck asked over the radio.

"Yes," I told him.

I had Nifedipine, Dexamethasome and Diamox. Nifedipine helps the lungs, Dexamethasome is for cerebral edema and Diamox helps one acclimatize better. I took each of the drugs. As I was administering these, I heard the radio conversation between Tucker in Base Camp and Jason in High Camp.

"If he doesn't get going, there's nothing we can do," Jason was saying. "He's got to move."

Here was a man who'd saved people high on the North Side of the mountain saying there's nothing they can do to help me. I knew he was right. He was well below us by then. But, deep down, I figured, "It's no big deal. I'll just sleep here for the night. I don't need any help. I'll feel better after I sleep."

Then it hit me.

"If I stay up here, I'll die."

I can understand how someone might just sit down, close his or her eyes, and never open them again. I was almost there. Until I started to realize I was blowing it.

I thought of Maggie and how unfair this would be to her. I thought about my business partners and how great everything was going at home. I felt as if I was leading a charmed life. I even thought, "I'm going to pick up my new

Cirrus SR22 plane when I get back." One of my major goals had been to climb Everest, but another had been to own my own airplane. It was about to be a reality.

"What's Maggie going to do with an airplane?" I thought.

I knew, financially, everything would be OK for her. I had life insurance. Maggie would be taken care of, but what about Mingma? That's what finally got me going again. I looked at him, waiting for me. I didn't know how long he would stay with me, but I guessed it would be too long. I figured I was compromising his safety, too. It was not fair to Mingma.

I looked up at that 60-foot vertical rise leading to the South Summit. There were two defined sections. I decided in my mind to climb the first one and see how I felt. Maybe then I'd try to climb the second one. If I could get to the top of the South Summit, I knew everything after that was down hill.

KEVIN, PLEASE ...

I took my first drink in four hours and hoped the medications would kick in. I started thinking that maybe I could do this; maybe I could at least climb back up to the South Summit. After that, it would be all downhill. Then I mentally admonished myself, "Just climb back up to the South Summit. Don't get ahead of yourself. Break it down into smaller pieces."

That's when Mingma looked at me with pleading eyes and said, "Kevin, please, we must go." It was typical, gentlemanly, warm Sherpa. He should have been shouting at me. Screaming and swearing. But, instead, he said in a pleading, even voice, "Kevin, please..."

It was a difficult ascent up to the South Summit. I had to rest all the way up. Normally, on descents I am steady and keep going forward. But this descent was going to be different.

Partway up the South Summit I needed a longer rest. After about a minute or two, I heard Mingma say again, "Kevin, please, we must go."

I would take three, four or five steps and rest for at least 15 seconds, sometimes longer. This would become my routine. Occasionally, when I lingered too long, Mingma would repeat, "Kevin, please, we must go."

I reached the South Summit and rested there for about 15 minutes. Then I stopped hearing my oxygen flow.

"Oh, darn it, my oxygen has run out." I said matter-of-factly, "Mingma, my oxygen is out."

He immediately unhooked my oxygen and took off his oxygen and gave me his bottle. He had no concern for himself. It wasn't even a discussion. I didn't ask for his oxygen. I didn't expect it. I sure as hell didn't deserve it. It was Mingma's decision and he made it immediately. He selflessly gave it over. On top of that, he didn't throw away the empty bottle; he put it in his backpack to carry down the mountain.

Then he looked at me and said, "Kevin, please, we must go."

HEADLAMPS AT THE BALCONY

I put one foot in front of the other. I was slipping. I would wrap my arms around the fixed ropes and slide down. When I fell on my butt, I would sit there for a moment. Ah, a rest. Mingma would give me 15 or 20 seconds and then coax me to continue.

"Kevin, please, we must go."

I felt the pinky on my right hand starting to get frostbitten. But I focused on the Balcony. I knew what was below me and because I'd been falling so much, I wasn't looking forward to the challenge ahead.

Mercifully, the weather was holding. It hadn't gotten windy or nasty. If the weather turned bad, I would be in serious trouble. But I never thought about that. Just one foot in front of the other. Slip, fall, rest, repeat.

Down and down we went. If I made 10 or 12 steps without slipping down or sitting, I was doing great. Then the light started to fade. It was turning to dusk. Afternoon had become early evening. We were making progress, but it still seemed impossibly far to go.

In my journal, I wrote:

It started getting dark around 7 p.m. and I got out my headlamp. Mingma had left his at the Balcony. I started to think about the un-fixed section I was going to need to negotiate. Climbing unroped in my stumbling condition didn't appeal to me—but I had no choice. Plus, I was seeing minor visual distortions. I could see some headlamps at the Balcony about 300 vertical feet below me and I figured Tucker had sent some Sherpas up to assist us. I was so tired as I approached the Balcony. I knew they would have O₂, but I prayed they brought a sleeping bag so I could bivy at 27,500 feet.

Had I been thinking clearly, I would have dug out my extra headlamp in my pack for Mingma. It never occurred to me. I guess I forgot it was there. Mingma had to descend behind me, using only the light from my headlamp.

I was thankful that Mingma would soon be getting a bottle of oxygen and I would get fresh Os and be able to breathe it at a higher rate.

We reached the unroped section. I was extra careful as we descended through this area. I negotiated it fine. Slow, but fine.

I would stop to rest, leaning over my ice ax, coughing. I was flat-out exhausted. I'd been going a long time, but I knew I should be feeling better than this. Finally, I saw the headlamps bouncing up toward us. IMG had its plan in place.

I felt badly that the Sherpas had climbed up there to help me. I knew I wasn't doing this climb with the style that I had wanted. I'd been late in reaching the summit and I had turned into a problem coming down. You want to be able to climb with some relative self-sufficiency.

I was greeted at the Balcony by the smiling Panuru.

"How are you doing?" he said, as if we were meeting on the street in Kathmandu.

"Do you have a sleeping bag?" I gasped.

"Oh, no, we're going down," he told me gently.

I was disappointed and thirsty. They had some hot tea for me. I was given a fresh bottle of oxygen and they turned the flow up pretty high. Mingma got a bottle, too. I wanted to rest, but they were stern about moving on. Mingma went ahead of us. Soon he was gone from my sight.

Tashi walked in front of me and Panuru was behind. I was able to move down the fixed lines, clipping and unclipping. There were some tricky parts, but it wasn't bad. I was so tired. I sat back down and started to slide. Panuru encouraged me to sit glissade.

We left the Balcony at 8:30 p.m. From there, it should be about an hour and 45 minutes to High Camp. Tashi was in front, followed by me, and Panuru was right behind me. The Sherpas couldn't understand why it was taking me so long. Tashi would look back up at me disgusted whenever I took a rest break. Panuru was much more forgiving. Whenever I looked back at him he just smiled and offered encouragement. I knew we were going to get down to High Camp; I wasn't concerned about that. It was just going to take a while. I would take five or ten slow steps and start to breathe hard.

Other climbers were coming up now. It was the next summit day already. I felt as if I was in college, where every once in a while I would get home late as everyone else in the house was getting up to go to work or school. I was pretty wasted, too. It was 10:15 p.m. Finally, I was reaching High Camp. I could see the tent only 50 yards away, but still I had to stop and rest.

High Camp was a welcome sight, but I wasn't euphoric. I knew I had two more days of descent and I had never, ever been this completely drained in my life.

When I made it to the tent I was at least able to take off my own gear and get into the sleeping bag under my own power. I was coughing to beat the band.

In my journal, I wrote:

We finally returned to High Camp at about 10:30 p.m. I was out almost 24 hours and it was good to be back. I crawled into the tent that I shared with Dan and Ron. My vision was kind of foggy, but I never went snow-blind. I spent a miserable night at Camp IV. I couldn't stop coughing and had a hard time catching my breath.

HIGH CAMP AT LAST

I thought, "Get back to High Camp and everything will be fine." I figured I would probably have a miserable night of sleep, but at least I'd get some rest.

When I climbed into the tent, Dan and Ron were there.

"Welcome back," Dan said.

We didn't exchange hugs and celebrate having summitted the Big E. We were just happy to see each other. It had been a long day.

Sherpa Ram Bahardur brought me some soup. I wasn't as thirsty as I should have been, which was odd since I had drunk so little.

I coughed all night. If Ron had been worried about my snoring when we were assigned the same tent after ascending to High Camp, he must have loved my coughing fits. It was an awful night. But, obviously, I was happy to be back. I was far from overjoyed about making the summit at that point. I was concerned about the next few days and getting back to Base Camp.

I'd heard about many people who'd dragged their butts back to High Camp and felt so much better the next day. I hoped that would be me in the morning.

Unbeknownst to me, Simo called Maggie after I returned to High Camp. It would be hours before anything would be posted on the Internet. He wanted her to know as soon as possible that I was down, especially since they'd been reporting on me coming down late, very slowly. If you read between the lines, it was a little scary. IMG's Dispatch on everestnews.com read:

Mark Tucker reports from BC at about 8:15pm NEPAL TIME with the update on the IMG summit bid. The word is that Dan, Ron, Brien, Jason and Karma Rita Sherpa are all back at the Col and that Kevin is still coming down. ...Kevin, who is reportedly doing OK, but is slow, is still on his way down with Mingma. Additionally, Tucker sent Panuru and Tashi Dorje (who had carried oxygen to the Balcony last night and stayed at the Col in reserve just for such an eventuality) back up to meet Mingma and Kevin with more oxygen and hot drinks and the four of them are now moving steadily down to the Col and are expected back there in a while.

It was a Saturday morning back in the States. Everyone assumes you're safe once you get back to High Camp. As did I.

THE LONG, SLOW TRIP TO BASE CAMP

The next morning dawned beautifully. I had barely slept and felt like death warmed over. I expected to feel better, but I didn't. Dan and Jason were geared up and ready to go down. I was getting it together, but moving in slow motion. We had big packs to carry down—all the gear you brought up and the oxygen, maybe 45 pounds. It wasn't ridiculous, but it was still 26,200 feet and the going was a little dicey. Tucker kept calling up on the walkie-talkie asking how I was doing and telling people to make sure I didn't carry too much. I wanted to carry my load. I wasn't doing this with style.

Everyone was happy. All the Western climbers and two Sherpas had made the summit. It was a huge success. It should have felt great. But it didn't.

Brien was a bit slow, too. We would later learn that he

had a touch of bronchitis. But he was nowhere near as slow as me. We took some photos, which I wasn't really interested in. The five Western climbers posed. Brien was shooting some video. Normally, I was super talkative and playing around, but I wasn't saying anything. I started out using supplemental oxygen, as did our entire group. I was confused that I was still feeling so pitiful. I was hoping that every step down would make me feel a little bit better.

Brien videotaped the Northeast Contingent summit team: Dan, Jason and me. We all put our hands in a circle. I put my hands in with the rest, but I didn't say anything. It was very unlike me. I wasn't celebrating. I didn't have any extra energy for anything.

When I hefted my pack on, I gasped. Either it was really heavy or I was really weak. Sadly, it was the latter. The first 20 minutes from the South Col to the top of the Geneva Spur is flat, but I was taking 20 steps and having to rest. I wasn't much better than the night before. I had a fever. A fever and descending Mount Everest was not a great combination.

Ram Baharadur, our cook at High Camp, was following us to the top of the Spur. Because I was so slow, they suggested I lighten my pack load. Reluctantly, I took out about eight or 10 pounds. Ram took a few of my non-essentials and returned to High Camp. Brien and Dan carried some of my stuff as well. I felt badly. Here I was being assisted. In the back of my mind, I was thinking I sucked. It wasn't fair to my teammates. This summit run lacked the elegance I would have liked. Even though you get a lot of support—with Sherpas carrying your oxygen and fixing lines—you want to be able to take care of yourself. I wasn't doing that.

The top of the Spur is a little scary. I rappelled down

using my belay device. I started feeling a little bit better, but I still had to rest frequently. I crossed the Traverse and headed down to the Yellow Band. Other teams were coming up toward the rocky section of the Geneva Spur, including our second wave of IMG climbers. I'm sure we looked haggard. All of us were beat up. But we were coming down successfully from the summit. All of those guys congratulated us. That actually propelled my spirits more than anything. I didn't feel great, but I was doing a little better. It was still a slow go to Camp 3. We'd been late leaving High Camp, probably around 10:30 a.m., so by the time we reached Camp 3 it was around 2 p.m. I got out of my down suit. I would descend in my Gore-Tex climbing bibs, which were more comfortable. Before leaving Camp 3, we melted snow for water.

Descending the Lhotse Face down to Camp 2, I was still feeling poorly. Usually, it was an hour down the Face and then another 30 minutes to Camp 2. This time it took at least twice as long. Jason stuck with me going down the Lhotse Face. It was very steep so I had gravity working in my favor, but I still had to rest frequently. (The downside of that gravity equation would be to miss a clip, slip and fall to your death.) Dan, Brien, Jason and I stuck together. It didn't surprise me that they were so supportive. I would have done the same for them. We all like each other. Ron had gone on ahead and alone. It took us a long time to go down, mostly due to my snail's pace. Camp 2 usually was comfortable, even though it was 21,300 feet. I figured I'd feel better than at High Camp; I'd be a mile lower.

I was aware that I needed to be extra, extra careful because I wasn't at the top of my game. I felt reasonably safe during the descent, just incredibly slow.

At the base of Lhotse Face, moving onto the Western Cwm proper, we still had a half-hour on reasonable snow slopes with crevasses. We roped up through that area. Brien and Dan roped together and Jason and I were together. The sun was going down behind the mountains. It was still light when we pulled into Camp 2 at 6:30 p.m. The half-hour descent took more than an hour.

I thought, "Great. Now I'll feel better." I kept waiting to feel better.

Even though it was 1,000 feet higher than Mount McKinley, Camp 2 was a comfortable altitude. Relatively speaking. I'd never slept on Os there. But we were fat on oxygen so they radioed us from Base Camp and told us to make sure we used the Os if we wanted. I expected to feel good that night, but I didn't. I shared a tent with Jason. I had shortness of breath and I couldn't stop coughing. I'd sit up and try to breathe. Sometimes it felt as if having the oxygen on made me cough more. I wasn't doing any better at Camp 2 than I was at High Camp.

I remembered thinking I needed to get through the night. I wanted to get to Base Camp.

Base Camp was usually the elixir of life. I hadn't slept much in several days. Friday night, I had gotten maybe three hours; Saturday night, three or four maybe; and Sunday about the same. I was really behind the curve as far as sleep was concerned. I tried to eat, but wasn't hungry. I drank some, but not the five or six liters I needed each day.

I was concerned. Actually, a little frightened. I realized I was sick. It wasn't just exhaustion from a long summit day. There was something wrong with me.

GROWN MEN CRYING

At breakfast the next morning, we were listening in on the radios for reports on the four other climbing members of the IMG team. Swee had reached the Balcony and turned around. He was attempting to summit without oxygen. He had already summitted Everest in '98 with oxygen. I thought climbing to 27,500 feet without supplemental Os was one hell of an accomplishment. Will and Brad had turned around, too. Will was using a different oxygen system than the rest of us and he had some problems with a freezing valve. So when Will turned around, his videographer Brad was obliged to spin as well.

Mike Donahoo was making his second summit attempt. He had made the Balcony several years earlier, but it didn't work out. He was doing OK this time, but he was moving a bit slowly. He was above the Balcony and a long way from the summit. I remembered overhearing the exchange on the radio. He knew it was late. Panuru was exhorting him, "Turn around, turn around. It's OK. The mountain will always be there."

You could hear how heartbroken Mike was. You could hear he was close to tears. I felt so much empathy and sympathy, having been there before. You put all that training and time, money and ego into it and then you come to the realization that it isn't going to happen. I felt a pang of guilt that my late-night performance might have rolled into the decision-making process. I wondered if they were thinking they didn't want another Kevin up there. He was around 28,000 feet when he made the courageous but heartbreaking decision to turn around. Most non-climbers don't realize that it's often harder to turn around than to keep on going.

It was hard to listen to that as we were headed down. I could feel his pain. We desperately wanted everyone to be successful. But I knew I couldn't dwell on it too much. I knew I had to get myself down to Base Camp.

Dan and Jason left before Brien and me. Brien said he wasn't feeling super fast so he would go with me. We had to carry more stuff because this was the last trip down and we had cached some gear at Camp 2. My pack was back up to 45 or 50 pounds. Brien and I headed down from Camp 2 to Camp 1. It was pretty easy the first two-thirds of the way, a gentle slope on the Western Cwm. There were a number of crevasses and ladder crossings approaching Camp 1. We had to rappel into a few crevasses and climb out of them. Normally it would take us about an hour; it took at least two hours. Everything took twice as long. After making Camp 1,

I knew we had to go through the Khumbu Icefall. I was not eager about this part of the descent.

We were told we could lighten our load at Camp 1 and leave some gear for the Sherpas, but I didn't unpack anything. It was a matter of principle, a matter of pride. I felt awful about my performance from the South Summit to the true summit and all the way back down. It made me mad. There was nothing I could do about it. I'm normally pretty strong and mentally tough, but I couldn't will myself to go faster. So I sucked it up and carried what was on my back. A small victory.

It clouded up as we went through the Icefall, which kept it from being super hot; a godsend. Brien was a good companion because he was going slower than normal so he wouldn't get annoyed with my pace. But in reality, he would have been accommodating regardless of how he felt. I was picking up snow and eating it to deal with the dryness in my mouth. It was a zombie-like descent. Six days earlier, we'd climbed up the Icefall faster than we were now climbing down through it.

I was looking forward to getting to that point in the Icefall where we would be past the objective danger. As spring headed toward summer, the icefall was falling apart. A lot of protection had melted out. We couldn't always count on the fixed lines toward the bottom of the icefall. I was thinking, "You can't screw up here. You're almost home." Usually, as I get closer to my objective, I feel that rush of adrenaline. My pace quickens. But I had none of that. I had to keep resting.

We were tired puppies coming down. We reached the base of the Icefall where it was normally an eight to ten minute walk across the moraine to our camp. We sat down and took off our spikes. All of the objective mountain danger was finally behind us. The route back to our tents wasn't completely straightforward. We tried to take the path of least resistance. It probably took 20 minutes. Finally, we saw our tents.

"Thank God," I thought. "We're back at Base Camp."

I knew now I wasn't going to die on Everest. I didn't kill myself. I'd come pretty close, but I was still alive. I just kept waiting for the switch to go on, to feel like myself again. But it wasn't happening.

PERMISSION TO FEEL GOOD

The rest of the team was in Base Camp when Brien and I straggled in. Out came Tucker. He couldn't have been happier to see us. He was probably relieved after what had happened over the past few days. But he exuded sheer joy at our success.

"Wait, wait," he said to us. "Put your arms around each other. I'm taking pictures."

All I wanted to do was sit my sorry butt down in the comfy mess tent chair and drink some hot lemonade. Brien is 5-foot-8 and I'm 5-foot-9, but in the photo that Tucker took I looked about three inches shorter than him. I was all hunched over. I probably weighed about 145 pounds at that point, easily 20 pounds less than when I began.

I was happy to be at Base Camp. I could finally stop

moving.

I was still coughing a ton and short of breath. After doing photos and getting us into the mess tent, Tucker said, "Hey, Kevin, I paved the way for you to visit the med tent. Let's just get you checked out. I hope that's OK with you."

"No problem," I said.

But first I needed to take a righteous schmoo. I hadn't gone No. 2 since Friday at High Camp. It was a full three days. On summit day, having to go to the bathroom can be a problem. Some people even take Imodium to avoid having to go. You don't want to be up high, wearing all that gear, and feel the need to go. In fact, it could easily ruin your summit attempt. But after getting back to Base Camp, it was pleasing.

After that, we slowly ambled over to the med tent. I hadn't even been to my personal tent at Base Camp.

I sat down on a stool and they looked me over. My temperature was 101 degrees. No wonder I was so lethargic. My O_2 saturation was in the low 70s, which was lower than it should have been. They listened to my lungs. It didn't sound good.

"You have pneumonia and maybe some HAPE," the doc said, meaning I showed symptoms of High Altitude Pulmonary Edema.

They had me lay down on a makeshift cot.

"Have you been drinking water?" they asked.

"Not much."

They put an IV in me. They looked at my arms. I have fat veins, the kind nurses love. But when they started sticking me, they couldn't find one.

"Must be thin because you're so dehydrated."

I received four liters of IV fluids overnight, but I never

really felt the need to urinate. I was pretty dehydrated.

I had an IV in my arm and an oxygen mask on my face. I looked like someone in a hospital ward. Brien was checked out. He had a little bronchitis, but he didn't get the cot treatment. He was just Everest beat-up. Me, I was much worse off.

I was still short of breath. I'd cough and cough. I could tell they were concerned.

I kept saying I was sorry I was such a burden. "I'm sorry to put you out." All these people had gone above and beyond. There were two doctors who attended to me, Denise Merritt and Dan Langell. I kept saying, "I did poorly. I'm mad at myself. I descended without style."

I was glad I made the summit, but I didn't feel good about it.

Finally, Denise said to me, "First of all, I don't know why you guys do what you do. I don't get it. But think for a minute. You just climbed Mount Everest and you descended all the way back to Base Camp on your own power with pneumonia. You know what, you should feel pretty good about that."

She gave me permission to feel good about what I had just done.

I know no one climbed the mountain healthy, but I think I climbed it unhealthier than most.

Tucker visited me at the medical tent about six times that day. Mingma came to look in on me. He was wearing a North Carolina baseball cap. He looked so much smaller than I remembered him on summit day. He seemed so much bigger and stronger up high.

At one point, they put me in a Gamov bag, a hyperbaric

chamber designed to simulate a lower elevation. It's like a coffin. Some people get claustrophobic. They talked to me about it and I figured, "I'll give it a try." After 20 minutes I was not feeling any better. It was hot. I was starting to get a little claustrophobic myself.

At some point during that evening, Denise said, "Do you have insurance for a helicopter evacuation to Kathmandu?" I didn't think so; I declined it from the American Alpine Club.

"We think you should get a better look at a hospital in Kathmandu. Would you be willing to pay for it?"

"Do you think it's necessary?" I asked.

"Yes," Denise said.

Well, who was I to say no? It hit me that I wouldn't get to trek out with my buddies. I was a little crestfallen. Later on, Dan, Jason and Brien packed up all my gear. I never went back to my tent.

I was finally able to urinate. I ate a little bit of food. Dr. Dan spent the night with me, monitoring me. He told me he slept maybe an hour that night while he kept watch. I had the best night's sleep in four days. With the medications and hydration, I started to feel a little better. I was still in slow motion, but I was feeling better.

You need good weather to get a chopper in. I was thinking, "How much is this going to cost?" Tucker was on the radio. Simo was on the phone in Seattle. They wanted to make sure they sent in the right type of chopper. They favored the smaller, more powerful helicopters used by the Nepali Army. I remembered looking at the helicopter crash site from the previous year, the wreckage of a big Russian M-16 model.

I would miss the trek out, but I'd done that before in 2002.

I called home on the sat phone and talked with Maggie. "You sounded terrible," she later said. I'm glad I didn't call when I was really feeling bad.

FIRST HELICOPTER RIDE

My buddies came out to see me off. They brought me a comfy chair to sit in at the helicopter pad. The Sherpa cookboys were out there tossing rocks around to make the landing pad more level. It was incredible to see everyone trying to help me out.

A month and a half ago, along with a bunch of other teams, I'd helped build this pad. I never envisioned I'd benefit from my labors.

A couple of guys, originally Americans, had chartered a chopper to come to Base Camp. Later, I found out they worked for Eagle Global Logistics (EGL), a shipping company. They had been investigating the opportunity of helping expeditions move gear and supplies into Nepal. Part of their due diligence was to check out Everest Base Camp via helicopter; a pretty sweet day at work if you ask me.

The chopper started coming in, circling. Then, suddenly, it left. The pilot was showing the passengers Base Camp, and then he dropped them at Gorak Shep. Plus, at this altitude, the pilot needed less weight in his aircraft. It was amazing watching the chopper come back and land. The pilot talked to Tucker for the longest time, then motioned me over. I brought my two big duffels. Because of the weather, he told me he could only take me as far as Namche Bazaar. It would get me down to 11,500 feet.

I wasn't sure what would happen in Namche. Maybe I would trek out from there. Maybe I would arrange for another chopper, which would be less problematic at the lower altitude. Oh, well. Faith in God, hope for the best, prepare for the worst.

So I got in the backseat of the chopper. It took forever for it to take off. I was aware of its lack of lift, but I was kind of numb to danger at that point and had no real fear. Brien shot video. On the videotape you can hear someone say, "Did you see that? They just barely got off the ground."

Shortly thereafter, we flew over the wrecked chopper, a grim reminder that we were right on the edge of the chopper's lifting ability.

It was a whirlwind. I'd been struggling to get down from the mountain. I was figuring on the decompression of the three-day trek out. Going from Pheriche to Namche and then to Lukla.

Once the chopper climbed to 500 feet above ground level, I felt more comfortable. I was actually enjoying my first helicopter ride. We passed over Gorak Shep. Minutes later we were flying over Lobuche. Then we turned left and headed down over Tuglha. A short while later we landed. But not in Namche.

The Nepali military pilot had landed in Pheriche at around fourteen thousand feet. "Bad weather in Namche at the moment," he explained. He instructed me to take my duffels out. Weight was still a huge issue for the chopper at this altitude. The pilot put in more fuel to go back and get the other two guys at Gorak. He said he'd come back for me and we'd then try to make it to Namche. But, with the weight of the two extra guys, my heavy duffels were no longer welcome on the chopper. I wasn't sure what was going to happen to me. I wandered around. I went to a teahouse and asked the owner if he could arrange for porters to take my duffels down to Lukla. It cost $120. Worth the price.

So I handed over $3,000 worth of gear to a total stranger, although I was not concerned. He was Sherpa. I trusted him. Plus, this was the same teahouse at which Stuart Smith and I took a rest break and drank Coke when we trekked out in 2002. It felt like good karma.

Sure enough, the chopper showed up again. The pilot got out to help me.

"How do you feel?" he asked.

"Well, I have pneumonia, not HAPE, so I don't feel that much better."

Typically, HAPE victims feel near immediate relief with descent of 3,000 feet or so.

"Did you make the summit?" the pilot wondered.

"Yes," I said.

He shook my hand, patted on the back and congratulated me with a warm smile. The pilot said he thought we'd be able to fly past Namche and all the way to

Phak Ding. The elevation of Phak Ding was just under nine thousand feet and it was relatively close to Lukla. When I got in the chopper with the two guys, they started asking me all these questions. I didn't mind.

We were flying down the valley formed by the Dudh Kosi, which, translated, means the Milk River, milky due to the minerals dissolved into the glacial melt. There were clouds well below the mountaintops. It was like flying through a triangular tunnel of visibility. We were in the clear in between the V-shaped river valley with the cloud ceiling only a few hundred feet above us. To pilots, this was known as "scud running," flying beneath a very low layer of clouds. Something I wouldn't do even over hospitable terrain. And we were scud running through the mighty Himalaya.

We were going to Phak Ding, through this "tunnel" and I was recognizing all the sights. We kept going past Namche. I thought we should be close to Phak Ding. It was raining a little bit. I was getting peppered with questions and I was happy to answer them because now I was the big Everest hero. At least that was what they thought. I knew better.

The next thing I knew we landed at the Kathmandu airport. It was 85 degrees and muggy. Apparently the weather was just good enough to make it all the way back to Kathmandu. I later learned that on that day there were four other choppers scheduled for flights within the Khumbu Valley. Ours was the only one to go.

The helicopter ride should have cost $5,000. But I was able to split some of the costs with the guys from EGL. It cost me $2,200.

I had no idea if I'd be met by anyone at the airport. The two EGL guys offered to give me a ride. But Kieran, a Nepali who worked for Great Escapes Trekking, which is associated with IMG, was already there with a driver. Just another reason why Eric Simonson is considered the best at logistics.

There was almost no traffic in the city. Apparently, a loosely organized bandh—a general strike—had been put in place by the Maoist insurgency. They took me to the Travel Medicine Center of the CIWEC Clinic.

A female Indian doctor named Prativa Pandey greeted me. "You're our Everest mountaineer. We've been waiting all morning for you."

She checked me over. There was some fluid in my right lung, but my vitals were pretty good.

"They gave you good medications on the mountain," the doctor said. "You're well on your way to recovery."

Actually, at Base Camp they gave me four liters of IV fluids, Ceftriaxone, Combivent, Servent, Nifedipine, OTC cough syrup, Diamox, Zithromax and Codeine.

Dr. Pandey gave me Zithromax and some cough suppressants.

"That's it," she said.

"That's it! I don't have to go to a hospital?"

"No. Just take one Zithromax today and one more tomorrow."

I walked out of the clinic. My amazing whirlwind was over. I was in Kathmandu after having been in Base Camp two hours earlier. Only three days before, I'd been on the summit of Mount Everest.

DON'T ROT IN KATHMANDU

I told Kieran what I'd done with my two duffel bags. He asked me what I wanted to do. What I really wanted was to go back to the Hotel Tibet, take a shower and get cleaned up. It was supposed to take four or five days for the duffels to get to Lukla and be flown back to me.

I asked Kieran if I should wait for the bags.

"You should definitely wait," he told me.

Crap. That was not what I wanted to hear. My problem was, I had no friends in Kathmandu. All my buddies were up at Base Camp. What was I going to do for four or five days? Oh, well, I figured it would help me decompress from the mountain. I'd find some books to read and hang out.

I took a shower and had a delightful lunch back at the hotel. Even though I shouldn't have, I drank a beer.

It was warm and humid. It was so nice to see the greenery of spring. Trekking out, when you get close to Lobuche, the spring flowers would be in bloom. There would be rhododendrons out in their full glory. I'd missed all that by flying out. Now I was enjoying what was around me.

To go from feeling so lousy and needing a helicopter ride to being in Kathmandu and not feeling totally awful was really weird. When I limped out in 2002 with my bad knee, I was so bitter and disappointed. Those three days of trekking soothed the rough edges. It was nice to be out in nature. It was so pretty that you had to say, "I didn't make the top, but look at how beautiful it is here." It's all part of the decompression process.

It was hard for me now to get my bearings. I talked to some people around the hotel. I took another shower. After nine weeks on the mountain, it just felt so good. I decided to watch some television. I hate to admit it, but there was a fashion show on. There were these gorgeous models. I had to stop and watch it a little. I'd seen some cute yaks, but nothing like that.

While I was watching the fashion show, the phone rang. It was the boys at Base Camp. They were using up my prepaid satellite minutes. It was so good to hear from them. I told them I was doing well.

"I'm sitting here watching supermodels on TV," I said. "How are things at Base Camp?"

We all had a good laugh.

What transpired on the mountain hadn't set in yet. All I knew was the danger was behind me.

The phone rang again about 20 minutes later. I thought it was the boys again, but it was Eric calling from Seattle.

I thought he was going to yell at me for bad decision making up there. Instead, he congratulated me. He was thrilled I was back down and safe. It was so good to hear from him. I have a tremendous amount of respect for Simonson. He was genuinely psyched for me.

"What are you going to do?" he asked.

I told him about my duffels. "I've got to wait for my bags."

"Hell, no," he said, "don't rot in Kathmandu. Go home. See Maggie. Get out of there. We'll figure out how to get your bags to you."

I had been given permission to go home. It was so cool to talk to him. After hanging up the phone, I went to sleep for the first time in a real bed, something I hadn't done in over two months. I was thinking about going home. Sweet dreams.

MORE TEARS AT THE AIRPORT

The next morning I called Great Escapes and said, "I want out." I love Nepal and the people, but I wanted to go home.

My plane ticket was for 10 days later. They said they could get me to Hong Kong through Bangkok, but they were booked for the rest of the legs.

I decided I would go for it and see how far I got. I'd been gone for two months and change, yet I would have no baggage to check, just a small carry-on knapsack. The desk attendant at The Hotel Tibet asked about my trip and offered profuse congratulations for making it to the summit and back down again.

I was really skinny. I put on the blue jeans I'd worn over. I had to cinch them up really tight—and they were still loose. I'd wanted to go to the Rum Doodle, but with the Maoist strike the driver suggested it wouldn't be a good idea. I thought, "That's too bad, but maybe I have an excuse to come back someday. It will be fun to sign my name on the wall along with so many other Everest summiters."

At the airport lounge, I was waiting and I started to write in my journal all the things that had transpired. I tried to remember all that I'd been through. One of my last worries was getting out of Nepal without any Maoist problems. When the plane left Kathmandu I knew that little hurdle was over. What a different feeling it was leaving now as opposed to last time. I had a warm place in my heart for the country, the people and the mountain. I had satisfying memories, even though I got my butt kicked.

When we landed in Bangkok, I went immediately to the Cathay Pacific Airlines counter to negotiate my return flights.

"We can get you to Hong Kong," she told me, "but there's no way we can get you back to New York until..." Clickity-click, she was typing on the keyboard. "Not tomorrow."

"Hmm," I was thinking, "I guess I can spend a day in Hong Kong. But I want to get home to see my wife."

Clickity-click, clickity-click.

"There are no flights available until yours on the 31st," I was told.

"Look," I said, a little upset, maybe pleading a little. "I've just been to the summit of Mount Everest and I'm pretty beat up."

It didn't take a lot to look pitiful.

Clickity-click.

"We have openings in business class," she said.

"How much?"

"$1,300."

The flight left the next day. I'd have to stay overnight in New York City, too. But I would take it.

I got a room at the Amari Hotel and ordered room service—steak and wine. I hung out in my room and relaxed.

I put on shorts and noticed for the first time the big bruises on my legs. All that falling and sliding down during the descent from the summit had left its marks.

When I'd headed for Everest in March, I was in the best shape in my life. Now my quads and pecs, which had been really built up, were all withered. After the body goes through the fat reserve, it starts to eat away at itself. It was amazing to take inventory of myself. "Man," I realized, "I got my butt kicked."

The next day, I flew from Bangkok to Hong Kong. It was only three hours and I was still seated in coach. But I was looking forward to riding in business class, a new world for me. I'd never ridden in anything but coach. Now I didn't have to hang with the other tourists. While I waited in Hong Kong, I was admitted into the fancy lounge. When I ordered a beer and went to pay for it, I was told, "Oh, no, that's covered."

Then life got really fun. I was still in a whirlwind fog. When we boarded the plane, the flight attendant said, "Right this way, Mr. Flynn." Oh, they knew my name.

I took a seat in a big, wide, soft leather seat. I couldn't even kick the seat in front of me. Just when I was thinking how much I was going to enjoy this, the flight attendant came to me and asked, "Some French champagne, Mr. Flynn?"

Why, of course, I've just climbed Mount Everest.

After taking off, I watched *Touching the Void* again. One of the few movies made about mountaineering that got it right. I ate a five-course meal. It was really good food for airline food. Of course, after what I'd been eating, anything was going to taste great.

There was vintage wine with every course. I didn't drink enough to get drunk, but I had a nice inner warmth. Dinner—and all the eating—took almost as long as the movie.

I was trying not to cough to avoid bugging the passengers around me. I felt safe, warm and comfortable. That's when I started to think about summit day. I was looking straight ahead, smiling. I couldn't shut my eyes. If you were sitting next to me you would have thought I was an idiot. I sat for the next eight hours staring straight ahead, smiling, re-running the hard drive in my mind, replaying the tapes of summit day. I had a hard time believing it really happened. It was almost like a dream that was too good to be true. Maybe we stopped at a false summit. Did it really happen? I couldn't believe it happened. I felt such a profound happiness and appreciation for what had occurred.

Hour after hour passed with me grinning at the thought of what had happened. It could have been so much better, but it worked out. "You undeserving amateur, you somehow snuck up on Mount Everest and made the top—and made it back alive." Maybe my ego was taking over, but to get down with pneumonia, I figured the doctor was right. I should feel good about getting up and down.

Here I was on a plane and my buddies were still in Base Camp.

Before we arrived in Vancouver, the guy next to me

struck up a conversation. On my other trip back, I almost didn't want people to ask me where I'd been. Now I wanted people to ask.

When we landed in Vancouver, I called Maggie and we talked for forty minutes. I was in North America. We were on the same continent.

I flew to New York City and spent a night at a hotel. The next morning I flew back to Rochester. When I got into the airport, my brother Chris and Ray Martino had arranged for a homecoming with family, friends and media—reporters from TV, radio and the newspaper. They'd made a big poster at work. It said, "Nice ascent, Kevin." I walked down the jet way past the last security into my wife's open arms. She was crying. Again, there were tears at the airport.

THE TRUE HEROES OF EVEREST

I know in my heart of hearts I would not have had the confidence to carry on without Mingma's encouragement on summit day. He and I were the last ones left on the mountain that day. I would have turned around. But, more importantly, without his support I'm not sure I would have gotten down. I might have stayed up there. He was my guardian angel and my friend and he never yelled at me. God bless him.

The real heroes of Mount Everest are the Sherpas. Sherpa is not a job description; it's a people. Many Sherpas use their ethnic group as a last name.

Tenzing Norgay, as noted, was the first to summit Everest, along with Sir Edmund Hillary—though it was usually thought of as being the other way around, if one thought of Norgay at all. Everyone remembers the New Zealand explorer Sir Edmund Hillary, but they should also remember Tenzing Norgay. In 2003, the 50th anniversary of Norgay and Hillary's first ascent, Norgay's grandson, Tashi Tenzing, asked the mountaineering world to stop viewing Sherpas as "mere load-carriers and nameless catalysts to Western success."

From the first ascent in 1953 through the year I climbed Everest (2004), there were 1,584 people who stood on the top of the world, a great number of them were Sherpas. About 180 people died trying or while climbing down. Again, a great number of them were Sherpas. Fewer climbers likely would have made the ascent and more would have died if not for the Sherpas.

Mountaineers who have been to Nepal or Tibet and worked with the Sherpa people will never forget them. For many reasons.

First, there's their physical strength. Many are short of stature—usually about 5-foot-4 or 5-foot-5 and weighing 130 or 140 pounds—but they are so strong. Not only do they have enormous strength, they're also fast. Up high, when you ask how long something will take, you have to say, "Not Sherpa time, Western time." If they say four hours Western time, it will take a Sherpa about one and one half hours. Our final summit run and descent was accomplished over seven difficult days. Pemba Dorje Sherpa holds the Everest speed record. It took him only 8 hours and 10 minutes to reach the summit from Base Camp. Beyond amazing.

Secondly, I have found that almost all Sherpas are incredibly friendly people with warm personalities.

Sherpas climb because it's a job. It has made them famous. Not as famous as Western climbers, but famous in their own right.

Even though they're revered in Nepal, it's dangerous work. Many do it so they can send their children away to school in Kathmandu to get an education and, they hope, better and safer jobs.

Ask a Sherpa, "Do you want your sons to follow in your footsteps?" and they'll say, "Oh, no."

They don't climb Everest for the love of mountaineering, the way we do. But they are studs. Lance Armstrong is an amazing athlete and I look at the Sherpas in that light. They put in the fixed lines and do the hard work.

Securing ladders, fixing ropes, carrying oxygen bottles and some of the Western climbers' gear is a high-paying job by Nepali standards. They earn $2,000 to $3,000 during the three-month climbing season plus a reasonable equipment stipend, which is a lot of money in their country. Nepal's per capita income is less than $1,200 U.S. I paid Mingma an additional $1,000 for his support on summit day, twice the required amount. But he deserved more, much more. He has my undying appreciation and respect.

THAT GUY WHO CLIMBED EVEREST

Truth be told, the line between success and failure is razor thin. The decision I made in 2002 to stay at High Camp made a lot of sense. Sometimes it's harder to turn your back on the summit than it is to carry on. I actually made a smart decision. But that's not what I always heard. For example, from the customs guy at LAX, I heard, "Oh, you were right there. You should have gone for the summit." And I could almost hear him thinking, "Wow, what a wuss."

In 2004, I made the summit and I came desperately close to taking the big ice nap. But now I get slapped on the back. "Great job. Wow, you climbed Everest. That's amazing." Some of those same folks could have been consoling Maggie, the grieving widow, and then under their breathe saying, "What an idiot he was. How could he do that? What was he thinking? What a selfish S.O.B."

My decision-making in 2002 was probably better than in 2004.

It's like flying an airplane. You land in nasty weather, maybe weather that was much worse than the forecast and you feel pretty good about yourself. But if you crash, it's called "pilot error." That's a big mistake. A costly error. Especially if it costs your life. Or worse, the lives of your passengers.

In business, when you take some risks and things work out, you're smart. People marvel at your business acumen. If you fail, you're bankrupt. People marvel at your stupidity.

The higher you go, the farther you have to fall. Maybe that's what is so alluring about Mount Everest. The risk and the reward are both so great. I believe the same is true for flying and business.

After I returned in May 2004, I was that guy who climbed Everest. So many people know me that way now. I'm OK with that. Everyone wants to talk about it, and I never get tired of it. In 2002, I got tired of it very quickly.

Being that guy who climbed Everest has led to many different things including talking to kids and making motivational speeches for companies. I did an advertisement for Blue Cross/Blue Shield, the health insurance company that picked up the $2,200 tab for my helicopter ride, plus another $700 of cost from Everest Base Camp Medical and the CIWEC Clinic in Kathmandu. I was able to give back financially to the Everest Base Camp Clinic. I went back to Cornell University to speak. Then I was named the 56th Annual Rochester Press-Radio Club's Amateur Athlete of the Year. It was the first time a mountaineer had been recognized and it was the club for which my dad had been one of the founding members and the longtime master of ceremonies. As a boy, I dreamed of being a pro baseball player and receiving the Pro Athlete of the Year Award from my dad. I wished he could have been there to share in the moment, but, in my heart, I know that he was by my side. To me, he will always be "The Man of the Hour."

In May 2005, I was asked to give the commencement speech at Finger Lakes Community College. Looking into the shell at the Finger Lakes Performing Arts Center, I got to speak to 2,500 people about my passions. I recalled how Finger Lakes Community College was where I first came alive. My passion for education began there and it led to all these different places, including the summit of the highest peak in the world.

I quoted Howard Thurman, who said, "Don't just ask what the world needs. Ask what makes you come alive and then go and do it, because what the world needs is people who have come alive."

I came alive. I became well educated, an amateur mountaineer, a pilot, an entrepreneur. I became that guy who climbed Everest.

Postscript:
The Goodness of So Many People

People climb for a lot of reasons, but camaraderie is a big thing for me. There are horror stories of what people do on mountains, especially on Everest, which is notorious for attracting unfeeling, uncaring people who step over the dead and dying to reach the summit. I never ran into anyone like that. I found mostly great people there.

I have been with more than a few of them. I heard from them after returning from Everest—both when I failed to summit and when I reached the top. There were those who cared for me during and after my descent. Even though I kicked Mark Tucker's butt in card games, he was still great to me. I know he was watching out for me from Base Camp. Eric Simonson was watching over us from Seattle. I was moved that he called me at the Hotel Tibet with heartfelt congratulations.

He's one of my heroes in the mountains, so that meant a lot to me. I later found out that he had called Maggie as soon as I was safely back at High Camp. Everestnews.com had reported the rest of my team was back in High Camp and that "...Kevin is moving slowly but is OK." So Eric's prompt call to Maggie assuaged her concerns for my safety. I loved him for doing that. It's harder for those at home when they don't know what's going on. In the mountains, no news is good news. That may be easy to say but harder to accept if you're the one who is waiting at home.

I am grateful to the cook boys who helped out on the helicopter pad and the pilot who flew me to Kathmandu. And there were the guys with whom I did most of my climbing: Jason, who was exceptional; Dan, who was warm and funny and a great climbing partner; and Brien, who was on the same schedule because we'd both been sick when we first got to Base Camp. Brien and I climbed together on every trip up and down that mountain. It would be hard to ask for finer companions than Jason, Dan and Brien. They were strong and bright—and also great wise guys who knew how to pass time well. Stuart and Ted, from my first Everest expedition, did the same with and for me. There was a lot of down time on my expeditions to Everest, so enjoying the company of my teammates was very important to me.

Some people are truly solo climbers. There are very few on the 8,000-meter peaks. I'm in awe of those solo climbers— it's amazing they have that strength and wherewithal—but I like the fraternity of mountaineers. There's a special club that no one else gets admitted into. Jason, Dan, Brien and I are in a club that will carry on throughout our lives. Nothing can ever take that away.

When I got home, I received dozens of congratulatory cards, emails and phone calls. One of my favorites was from Phil Ershler. Phil and Susan Ershler are two of the finest people I've ever had the pleasure of meeting in the mountains, or anywhere else for that matter. Phil wrote:

Kevin:

Happiness is Everest in your rear view mirror. Big mountain, huh? Sue and I were super happy to hear of your success. Guess the hat worked. I trust you're feeling well. Heard the lungs weren't fully cooperating when you returned to base. Hell, it was time to go home anyway. Congratulations, amigo. We're proud of you Kevin.

Phil Ershler

He sure was right about Everest in the rear-view mirror. I had the "reindeer copulation" hat dry cleaned and promptly sent it back to Phil. I'm confident he'll pass the hat, with all that good karma, along to someone else.